ART COLLEGE ADMISSIONS

AN INSIDER'S GUIDE TO ART PORTFOLIO PREPARATION,
SELECTING THE RIGHT COLLEGE AND GAINING ADMISSION
WITH SCHOLARSHIPS

Art College Admissions
First edition, 2012

Produced by
W&J Publishing House
New York, NY

Copyright © 2012

© **Text**
Wook Choi

© **Photographs of Artworks**
Licensed under Oogie Art®. All rights reserved.

© **Non-artwork Photographs**
Certain photographs are covered by Creative Commons® Attribution Sharealike Licenses cited at the end of this book. All rights reserved.

Senior Designer
Justin Rhee

Assistant Designer
Yuri Hwoang

Editor
Justin Rhee

Distributor
W&J Publishing House
10 E. 33 St. 3 Floor
New York, NY 10016
United States
(212) 714-1011

ISBN 978-0-9855809-0-2
Printed in the United States.

"Oogie Art" is a registered tradmark of Oogie Art, Inc.

ART COLLEGE ADMISSIONS

AN INSIDER'S GUIDE TO ART PORTFOLIO PREPARATION,
SELECTING THE RIGHT COLLEGE AND GAINING ADMISSION
WITH SCHOLARSHIPS

WOOK CHOI

W&J PUBLICATIONS
NEW YORK

Dedicated to my son, Aron, my daughter, Aileen

&

The entire Oogie Art family

PREFACE

After earning my undergraduate degree in Fine Arts from Hong-ik University in Korea and my masters degree from New York University, it's taken me close to 20 years to come up with what I call the 50/50 approach to art portfolio preparation and art admissions.

To create the 50/50, I've spent thousands of hours over the course of my 28-year teaching career identifying (and testing) the most effective methods for art portfolio preparation in the US versus methods prevalent in Asia.

What may separate my approach from other approaches could be the fact that I have travelled not only the path of an educator, but I have lived the life of an artist as well.

I have often reflected as an educator on my experiences as an artist while helping students prepare their art portfolios and have felt blessed to have been born with what I, at times, have thought was too curious of a mind.

Years of not settling on a singular approach to art-making, I've realized, has empowered me as an art instructor with ideas that are free-form and almost always beyond the constraints of a particular set of histories or media.

Perhaps as a result, my students have gained admission to some of the world's most highly-ranked schools with over $28 million in scholarship awards.

I've distilled many of the principles underlying the 50/50 approach that I've advised those exact students with into the tips, case studies, and artwork images you'll find presented in this book.

In the first half of this book, you'll learn how vital a role art plays in the success of businesses today, what admissions committees at top art colleges really look for when deciding who to admit, and essential tips for developing winning art portfolio pieces.

In the second half, you'll learn about the distinct advantages and histories of the most highly-ranked and popular art colleges in the Northeast, specific and actionable tips for getting into each school, and any changes these schools have made to their admissions criteria in recent years.

You'll also come across images of my students' artworks throughout the book, which I've included to illustrate the amount of dedication, focus, and creative talent you should expect to exhibit in your own pieces to gain admission to and win scholarships from the schools featured in this book.

In the end, I decided to share the 50/50 only after having advised over a thousand students and parents to admissions and scholarship success because I believe it's an approach that can qualitatively change the way students and parents approach art portfolio preparation and the college application process.

In reading this book, I also hope that you gain more insight into the mechanisms of art college admissions, are encouraged to solve problems more creatively, and find the courage within yourself to develop the artistic talent that lies, I know, untapped in you.

A tremendous amount of research, planning, and collaboration went into the making of this book and none of it would have been possible without the kind-hearted generosity of the following individuals: Yuri Hwoang, my assistant designer, who taught herself Adobe InDesign for over a year just to help me create this book; Justin Rhee, for seeing this project through to its completion; Jang Myung Sool of

Boston Korea for allowing me to share my teaching experiences as columns in Boston Korea publications; Angiola Churchill, a great educator, for acting as a mentor to me all these years; Judy Collischan, Phoebe Zheng and Sun Can for their unflagging support and faith; Alex Tapnio, Lisa Feitel, Scott Larner, Tara Welty and everyone else from Scholastics for always supporting Oogie Art and its students; The Korea Times and The Korea Daily for their constant coverage and support of my students' accomplishments; Marisa Chearavanont and the Build Foundation for opportunities to work together in Northern Thailand; Lillie Wong, Daniel Vello, and the children of the Rumah Wawasan Homes in Malaysia for opportunities to work together in Ipoh, Malaysia; my students who helped to provide photos of their campuses and artwork images for this book; the National Foundation for the Advancement of Arts, Richard P. Mills, Former First Lady Laura Bush, Michael Bloomberg, and Congress Member, Jerrold Nadler for their support of my school, Oogie Art; my mother for always leading by example; and, of course, the continued support and encouragement of all Oogie Art students and parents.

I feel blessed to know you all and hope we can combine our creative energies over the course of several projects in our lifetimes to effect lasting and positive societal change.

CONTENTS

ON APPLYING TO ART COLLEGES

Why Art & Design Matter (Now More Than Ever)	21
Tips for Finding a College Match	31
Considerations in Choosing an Art College	41
Top 5 Tips For Art Portfolio Development	51
Art Portfolio Submission Tips & Guidelines	61

ON SELECTING THE RIGHT PROGRAM

The Cooper Union	73
Rhode Island School Of Design	83
Cornell University	95
Pratt Institute	107
Parsons New School For Design	119
The School Of Visual Arts	131
Carnegie Mellon University	143
School Of The Art Institute Of Chicago	157
New York University	169

1

WHY ART & DESIGN MATTER
NOW MORE THAN EVER

> " DESIGN ELEVATES BRANDS, SIMPLIFIES TECHNOLOGY, CREATES EFFICIENCY, AND INVIGORATES OUR PHYSICAL WORLD. AND IT IS BUT ONE DIVISION IN THE VAST LANDSCAPE ENCOMPASSING COLLEGE ART MAJORS TODAY. "

WHY ART & DESIGN MATTER
NOW MORE THAN EVER

The early 1990's was an era dominated by electronics behemoths like Sony and Panasonic. At the time when Lee Gunhui was president of a then obscure South Korean company, Lee committed himself to overhauling conventional business models through his massive "new management overhaul" starting in 1993, placing heavy attention on design and marketing in the coming years.

Samsung Smart TV on display at CES 2012.

At his company's 2006 keynote address, Lee said, "In the past, a company only had to create a good product in order to be number one; but the 21st century demands a product is properly designed, marketed, researched and developed in order to be the best." That little company has become quite a big player in the global market, dominating flat-screen TVs and cellular phone markets. Without Lee's respect for design, Samsung Electronics might have remained tucked away in South Korea.

Another of today's leading technology powerhouses shows the utmost respect for superior design. Far from being the final coat of paint after all the technological wizardry is achieved, design has always been at the very core of Steve Jobs' philosophy for Apple products. When Jobs first unveiled the iMac computer back in 2000, he said in Fortune magazine:

"In most people's vocabularies, design means veneer. It's interior decorating. It's the fabric of the curtains and the sofa. But to me, nothing could be further from the meaning of design. Design is the fundamental soul of a man-made creation that ends up expressing itself in successive outer layers of the product or service."

He further elaborated on design in Newsweek when discussing his 5th generation iPod:

"Look at the design of a lot of consumer products—they're really complicated surfaces. We tried make something much more holistic and simple. When you first start off trying to solve a problem, the first solutions you come up with are very complex, and most

On two occasions, Steve Jobs has called the iPad the "most important product" he has ever worked on.

Coco Chanel demonstrating how a sleeve construction with a high armhole permits freedom of movement without lifting the hem of a jacket.

La Marie Ghost Chair By Philippe Starck.

people stop there. But if you keep going, and live with the problem and peel more layers of the onion off, you can oftentimes arrive at some very elegant and simple solutions. Most people just don't put in the time or energy to get there. We believe that customers are smart, and want objects which are well thought through."

Apple painstakingly commits to this philosophy of design that results in the overall gestalt of a device. The only thing we consumers experience is a simple, sleek, and elegant gadget born from meticulously-planned design. As a testament to the success of the company's core values, Apple reports that it has sold over 108 million iPhones worldwide since its introduction in 2007.

But what good is a handheld device without the use of our hands? Coco Chanel is responsible for not only transforming black from somber to chic, but for also liberating the hand that was once a slave to the accessory. She is today credited for having designed an intuitive solution for the frustratingly occupied hands: the double-chain shoulder strap. And like all good design, it remains prevalent in our society while being so intuitive it appears invisible to the user.

Bilbao, Spain, on the other hand, in the early 1990's was a city on the brink of

Almost from the moment it opened in 1997, Frank Gehry's Guggenheim Museum Bilbao, with its distinctive titanium curves and soaring glass atrium, was hailed as one of the most important buildings of the 20th century.

being deserted due to its floundering economy. In an effort to revitalize the city through cultural infusions, renowned architect Frank Gehry was brought in to design the Guggenheim Museum Bilbao. Using titanium, he stripped the material of its previous associations – as dense, sturdy, mechanical – and used it to sculpt the museum into an organic, flowing whole, a fitting analogy for the city itself. The result was a structure so mesmerizing that it revitalized the city's economy through tourism, transforming Bilbao from a struggling industrial city into an artistic mecca.

Design elevates brands, simplifies technology, creates efficiency, and invigorates our physical world. And it is but one division in the vast landscape encompassing college art majors today.

With colleges supporting over 200 majors in the arts alone, emerging new fields of technology-related art studies, and a strengthened emphasis being placed on design across all industries, now is the best possible time for you to encourage your child to pursue the arts.

2

TIPS FOR FINDING A COLLEGE MATCH

> " RATHER THAN RELY ON RANKINGS, IT'S BETTER TO CONSULT AN ART TEACHER WHO NOT ONLY KNOWS A STUDENT'S PERSONALITY, STRENGTHS, AND POTENTIAL, BUT ALSO HAS A SOLID UNDERSTANDING OF EACH ART COLLEGE'S PROGRAMS. "

TIPS FOR FINDING A COLLEGE MATCH

Every year, US News releases its "Best Colleges" list, which ranks schools based on such factors as enrollment, faculty, tuition, room and board, SAT and ACT scores, admissions criteria, graduation and retention rates, college majors, faculty, school finances, activities, sports, and financial aid.

Harvard University's graduating class of 2010.

The list is great for providing broad profiles of top tier institutions, but does little to show how well a student's individual strengths and goals match a given school. For instance, RISD is ranked higher than Parsons on US News' scale, but Parsons is known as the top fashion program among art schools (while on this topic, it should be noted that SVA and Cal Arts are renown for their animation programs, while Pratt is excellent for architecture and interior design). With over 200 majors in the arts alone, the rankings do little to show which college has the strongest individual programs for specific fields and concentrations.

Rather than rely on rankings, it's better to consult an art teacher who not only knows a student's personality, strengths, and potential, but also has a solid understanding of each art college's programs.

Students who know their artistic goals should opt for an art college, where the first year is spent drilling foundations and the next three years are devoted to exploring one's concentration.

If, however, a student has a broader range of interests in addition to art, such as business or psychology, a top tier university will prove a better fit.

An art teacher who knows the student and understands each school's programs can then narrow down the list of colleges to choices that best fit a student's needs.

The next step is to visit each campus and talk firsthand with admissions officers. The goal is to find out about financial aid and scholarship opportunities, facilities and equipment, faculty and alumni, and internships and

If you have trouble finding a mentor, try reaching out to friends and family. Within your extended network of contacts, look for a professional in your intended field of study who can provide you with targeted and experienced advice.

Make sure you visit your schools during weeks when classes are in session so you can get a taste of what life on the campus is actually like.

career support. Prospective students will want a school that offers studio space, gallery exhibitions, cutting edge equipment, and access to professors who are industry professionals. Such mentors will not only offer invaluable insight, but provide integral opportunities for jobs and internships (these talented individuals are highly sought after by more expensive private institutions, which is why students will want to research a school's grants and scholarships). Students should aim to emerge from college with impressive portfolios, solid resumes, and a network of contacts in their respective fields. These elements are essential to an art student's future success for jobs and continuing education.

At this point, students and parents will have a comprehensive understanding of the prospective colleges, but there's still one more consideration to take into account: a student's work ethic. No amount of prestige, expensive equipment, and adept professors can compensate for an individual's sense of responsibility, self-motivation, and time-management skills. Some individuals need the comfort of having family support nearby, while others only function in their pre-established home structures. If one does not honestly assess these personal dispositions, it can result in struggling with the heavy workload, and lead to possible drop-outs or expulsions.

Getting into a great school is not enough; students need to determine if they can flourish once there. Knowing the ins and outs of each art program, along with one's personality and characteristics, will lend to the most rewarding and beneficial college experience that can best prepare students for their future in art.

3

CONSIDERATIONS IN CHOOSING AN ART COLLEGE

> "WHILE COMPETITION HAS GOTTEN TOUGHER OVER THE YEARS, ADMISSIONS REQUIREMENTS HAVE REMAINED FAIRLY CONSISTENT, WITH THE BIGGEST CHANGES OCCURRING IN SUBMISSION FORMATS AND HOME-TEST THEMES."

CONSIDERATIONS IN CHOOSING AN ART COLLEGE

Applying to art colleges involves a bit more complications than simply putting together a portfolio (which is itself no easy task – most schools ask for fifteen to twenty pieces). While competition has gotten tougher over the years, admissions requirements have remained fairly consistent, with the biggest changes occurring in submission formats and home-test themes. Nevertheless, every art school program has its own unique standards; knowing them will help you cater your applications for each school.

The first thing to consider is what type of art program will best suit your needs. Art schools such as Parsons

"Dreamers" by Stella Chung, admitted to UPenn, Brown and Cornell with over $100,000 in scholarship awards.

and SVA place greater importance on talent, technique and ability, whereas Ivy league and top 20 universities look for an all-encompassing educational background. These programs take into account not only the quality of your portfolio, but your GPA, leadership roles, ricular activites, standardized ores, and volunteering efforts as well. This fundamental difference between art schools and universities will determine which of the two will better suit your artistic interests and goals.

This main decision effects the kinds of pieces you'll include in your portfolio. Although art colleges have their own specific requirements, they all request three to four observational pieces (not based on photographs or magazine images). On the other hand, Ivys and universities will not ask for these kinds of works. Assuming your artistic proficiency, universities place greater weight on the sophistication of your concepts and ideas. Technique is directly proportional to the amount of time invested in the skill, which art schools prefer, whereas originality and creativity come from a synthesis of one's environment and experience pool in spirit of the Renaissance Man, which top universities seek.

It should be noted that even among Ivys, each university maintains its own admissions standards. For example, Cornell's art department judges your

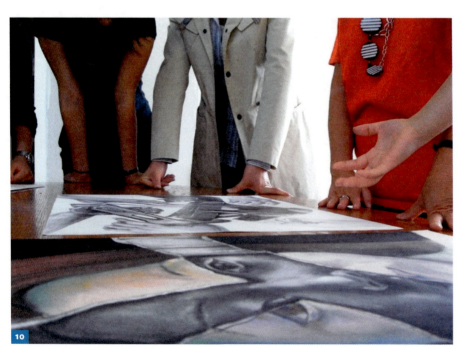

How you articulate the concepts, intentions, and processes underlying your work during your interview will have a major bearing on the way an admissions officer perceives your personality, character and aptitude.

portfolio separately from the rest of their non-art applicants. On the other hand, Yale will not give special attention to art portfolios, and will judge art program applicants under the same standards as all other applicants (and thereby increasing the difficulty in gaining acceptance).

Another factor to consider is the importance of the interview, which plays a critical role when top tier universities consider your application. The interview gives admissions officers a sense of your personality, character and aptitude – qualities that are impossible to reveal through transcripts and test scores alone. As such, make sure to schedule an interview with universities. If you're too far from the campus, there will most likely be an alumnus in your area who can conduct the interview closer to where you are. It's not guaranteed that the alumnus will have studied art, so prepare for the possibility of a broader range of questions that probe beyond art.

Tip! *Many schools strongly recommend you keep a sketchbook, and doing so can be an invaluable asset during your interview. If all is going well at your meeting, the admissions*

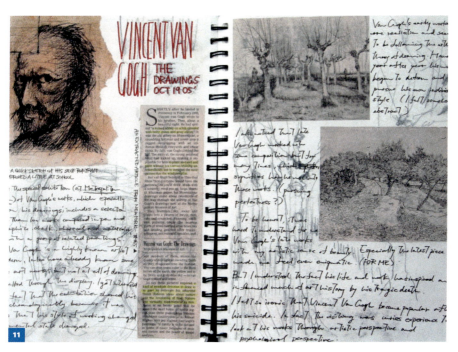

Presenting a developed sketchbook during your interview can give admissions committees further insight into how you think, investigate, and create.

CONSIDERATIONS IN CHOOSING AN ART COLLEGE – 43

"Physics of the Future" by Donna Cheung, admitted to Harvard University.

officer may ask to see if you have any other work besides your portfolio. At this request, you can take out your sketchbook, offer it to the officer, and reveal a deeper, richer side of you as an artist. This can leave a lasting impression.

If your interview goes well and you gain admission on the spot without having shown your portfolio, you will still want to send in your body of work if you're applying for scholarships. Allocation of grants and scholarships are determined by a different committee than your interviewer. When they consider your scholarship award, your portfolio will display a passion and commitment to your studies, and can increase the amount of scholarship dollars you are awarded.

Lastly, kindly seek out the advice of your high school's art teachers. They can help you prepare your portfolio and guide you towards a more dynamic education outside of the classroom. Teachers can help you setup your own show, inform you about art contests (to raise your profile and increase your chances for a larger scholarship), and introduce you to relevant artists and museums. However, you can always take initiative and fuel your own education by researching these things on your own; self-motivation will become an invaluable tool when you're left to your own devices in college.

TOP 5 TIPS FOR ART PORTFOLIO DEVELOPMENT

> " WITH THE TREMENDOUS SWAY YOUR ART PORTFOLIO WILL HOLD, IT WILL BE IMPORTANT FOR YOU TO STAY FOCUSED ON WHAT WILL BENEFIT YOU THE MOST IN THE LONG-TERM WHEN CREATING YOUR PIECES. "

TOP 5 TIPS FOR ART PORTFOLIO DEVELOPMENT

Although high standardized test scores and GPAs are vital for earning scholarships, art colleges have accepted applicants based on the strength of their art portfolios as well. With the tremendous sway your art portfolio will hold and the limited time you'll have to put one together, it will be important for you to stay focused on what will benefit you the most in the long-term when creating your pieces.

① **SHOW VERSATILITY AND RANGE**

Demonstrate a broad range of work and technical styles in your portfolio. Consider including drawings (black & white and color), paintings, collages, mixed media, sculptures, installations,

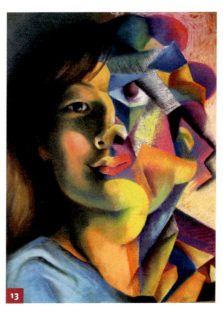

"The Metamorphosis" by Anne Park, admitted to Columbia University.

prints, photographs, and digital assemblages. By demonstrating technical proficiency across a wide range of mediums in your art portfolio, your work will convey that you've cemented a solid foundational understanding of basic art principles. This is important because the many major-specific concepts and skills art colleges look to teach you in your formative years as an undergraduate can only be fully actualized upon such a foundation.

Tip! *Unless if you are aiming to get into a more specialized or technical art college, avoid including too many works in your art portfolio that are specific to your intended major.*

② **EXPERIMENT AND EXPLORE**

Venture outside of your comfort zones by introducing new materials, techniques and ideas into your art every day. Explore your local art supply store for new tools and mediums, teach yourself a new Adobe Program or programming language, create an art installation, experiment with film and photographs, paint with your left hand, or alter newspaper clippings to define art on your own terms. Working in this way can help you discover new ways to express yourself and increase your chances of having your art stand out.

Tip! *Try looking for artistic potential in the objects and materials you come across at home and in your daily life. Who says you can't make art out of food, light bulbs, receipts, discarded*

"A Vignette of Addiction" by Kayeon Nam, admitted to Pratt Insitute with a $144,000 scholarship award.

items, books, nuts and bolts, magnets, or broken clocks? Keep an open mind.

③ **READ, READ, THEN READ SOME MORE**
Reading will empower you with knowledge, stimulate your imagination, and grant you more control over language. Not only will you have more ideas to work with for new pieces, you'll eventually be asked by colleges to write descriptions for each of your artworks (more on this later). How well you're able to articulate your intentions in this segment of the application process will indicate to admissions committees your communicative capacities as an artist, a thinker, and, most importantly, as a prospective student.

But! *Don't have the fear of getting rejected act as your sole motivating factor to read. Read to become a better communicator; read to establish yourself as more of an expert in your field; and read to keep your brain fit and your mind brimming with new ideas.*

④ **DELVE DEEPLY INTO THE TOPICS THAT INTEREST YOU THE MOST**
It's becoming increasingly important in this hyper-connected, tweet-by-the-second, touch-and-go age to learn how to still one's mind, cut distractions, and focus for extended periods of time on a single task or concept. Along the same line, be mindful of the overall impression your art portfolio may give off about you when it is viewed as a whole by an admissions committee. Though your art portfolio should reflect, first and foremost, a controlled understanding of foundational art techniques and

15

"Collapsed Perspectives" by Alex Khomyakov, admitted to RISD with a $92,000 scholarship award.

concepts, creating a series of works that center on a singular concept or visual theme can imbue your art portfolio with more intent and invigorate it with more purpose.

Tip! *If you're not sure where to start, try exploring specific memories and experiences, points of interest you've found in the work of others, current events that matter to you, or imagined futures.*

⑤ TALK AND WRITE ABOUT ART

Visit museums. Follow art, design, and architecture blogs. Share your experiences, findings, and reflections with others so that you can familiarize yourself with the language of art criticism. This will be important for when you present your work to college representatives in written statements, in-person meetings, and phone interviews. The more comfortable you are talking about art in general, the more comfortable you'll be when the time comes to present your own art.

Tip! *Not sure where to begin? Try starting a club at school, creating a Tumblr, writing an art review for your school newspaper, or joining museum and art gallery forum discussions.*

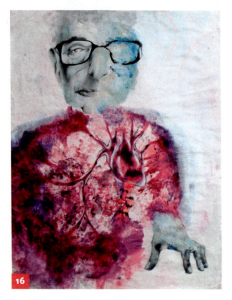

"The Bedeviled Heart" by Joel Tschong, admitted to Parsons with a $92,000 scholarship award.

5

ART PORTFOLIO SUBMISSION TIPS & GUIDELINES

> " THOSE WHO CAN EXPRESS THEIR IDEAS WITH CLARITY, PURPOSE, AND HONESTY ARE THE ONES WHO CRAFT GENUINE, AUTHENTIC, ORIGINAL PORTFOLIOS THAT WIN SCHOLARSHIP AWARDS AND GAIN THEM ADMISSION TO THE WORLD'S MOST HIGHLY-RANKED UNDERGRADUATE PROGRAMS. "

5

ART PORTFOLIO SUBMISSION TIPS & GUIDELINES

Keeping the following tips in mind when the time comes to submit your art portfolio will give you an edge over the competition:

SELECT THE RIGHT PIECES

Your art portfolio should consist of 15-20 artworks that you feel best communicate your creative voice, talent, and growth in the visual arts over the past 2 years. When making your selections, remember, always favor quality over quantity.

"In The Shadows" by Tanya Chearavanont, admitted to UPenn, Barnard and New York University.

Did you know? Certain colleges (e.g. RISD, the Cooper Union and others) will also require you to send shots of pages from a sketchbook to get an idea of how you investigate.

SKETCHBOOK TIPS

Make your sketchbook your own. For example, you can collage in magazine clippings, photographs, receipts, or,

, ticket stubs – maybe you can collect ticket stubs from events you've attended and then create an artwork in your sketchbook out of them. Just do your best to experiment, show creativity, and express your interests. Think of your journal or sketchbook as a repository and exploratory space for new ideas, a testing ground for new materials and techniques, and as a creative diary for your current interests. You don't have to keep it looking brand new, either, it's OK to get messy!

PHOTOGRAPH YOUR SELECTIONS

Preferably using a dSLR, photograph each of your artworks in a well-lit, white-walled setting at high resolutions for the best possible image quality. It could also help you to save each of your photographs in RAW formats to give yourself maximum flexibility when working with your images. For more information on the RAW format and its advantages, visit: http://en.wikipedia.org/wiki/raw_image_format.

ENHANCE YOUR ARTWORK IMAGES

Use Adobe Lightroom® or Adobe Photoshop® afterwards to enhance each of your images and to confirm that the resolution of each of your images

"Elderly Embryonic Figures Trapped by the Limitations of a Progressively Confining Illness" by Alicia Valencia, admitted to Stanford University and Brown+RISD's 5-year Dual Degree Program.

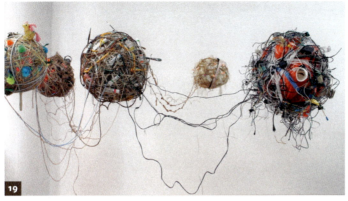

"Nebula" by Ada Blecher, admitted to Parsons with a $78,500 scholarship award.

meet's your intended school's DPI requirements. Some possible settings you can play with in either program include cropping your image to remove unsightly edges, leveling to achieve optimal contrast, and curving to fine-tune the colors in your images to make them as life-like as possible. Don't overdo it though, or admissions officers will take note.

Both Lightroom® and Photoshop® are available for free as trial versions on www.adobe.com.

ARRANGE YOUR PIECES EFFECTIVELY

Next, you'll need to decide on the order in which you'll present your pieces.

For the more general art portfolio, I recommend that you arrange your artworks by genre, starting with drawings, moving onto paintings, then mixed media, and so on. Aim to communicate in full the growth you've undergone as a young artist during this part of the process.

For the more conceptually-themed art portfolio, think about the way artworks are presented in an art gallery, then aim to create the same amount of visual continuity, conceptual coherence, and investigative progression.

WRITE INFORMED AND PERSONAL ARTWORK DESCRIPTIONS

Afterwards, I strongly recommend you opt to write 3-5 researched and well-written sentence descriptions for each of your pieces. Taking the time to write about the techniques, materials, ideas, and influences that underlie your pieces can serve to show admissions officers just how driven, informed, and promising you are as a visual artist, which can potentially tip final admissions and scholarship decisions in your favor.

CHOOSE A SUBMISSION METHOD

Locate on your intended school's site what options you have when it comes to submitting your art portfolio. You'll find that it usually boils down to one of the following three options.

① **PRINTS SUBMISSION OPTION**

Students who apply to Architecture programs or non-art colleges are usually asked to submit their art portfolio as photographic prints. When doing so, it's crucial you use Adobe Photoshop® to check that your image resolutions are close to 300 DPI, or dots-per-inch, as more DPI often equates to more details captured in your print.

Also, instead of ordering your prints from a Kinko's® or Staples Copy & Print Center®, which can diminish months - sometimes years - of hard work, maximize your chances by spending a few more dollars to have your artworks printed at a professional color lab. Matte or glossy prints don't matter so much

"Perceptual Contrast" by Hannah Kim, admitted to Carnegie Mellon University with a $70,000 scholarship.

as the weight of the paper your artwork photographs are printed on. Select a heavy paper (that's no larger than 8.5" x 11" or 21.5cm x 28cm each) and ensure that the printers use archival inks.

② **SLIDEROOM**

Although converting photographs into slides – think slide projectors – was the preferred method for art portfolio submissions in the 90s, smart web app developers from Carnegie Mellon U. released in 2006 an online art portfolio submission review tool known as Slideroom, which has quickly become the preferred method for managing art portfolio submissions for major art colleges including CMU, RISD, SVA, Parsons, and Pratt, among many other schools.

Slideroom is fast, intuitively-designed, and easy to use. A major advantage of using Slideroom instead of creating photographic prints is that after you've prepared one art portfolio for submission, Slideroom gives you the option to you easily duplicate that submission for your other intended colleges, saving you time and possibly hundreds of dollars in printing costs. Detailed instructions for using

"A Portrait in Beans" by Celina Greene, admitted to SMFA at Tufts University with a $104,000 scholarship award.

Slideroom are available on Slideroom's site (www.slideroom.com). Be aware that you may be charged $10 for each Slideroom submission depending on your list of intended schools.

③ **CD/DVD SUBMISSION OPTION**

If you choose to send your portfolio directly to your intended school on a CD/DVD, you should submit photographed 2D/3D works as separate .JPG files and time-based or performative works as .MOV or .MPG files – do not combine your images/videos in presentations or slideshows of any kind (e.g., PowerPoint or KeyNote). Also, ensure that none of your image files exceed 3MB – this reduces load times for admissions officers – and make an effort to include a printed thumbnail page showing all the images you've burned on your CD/DVD.

Whichever submission method you pick, you must include a work description sheet. Number the artworks you're submitting and list the corresponding number, medium, size, date of completion and title for each work on your description page. You could even include image thumbnails of your artworks in your work description sheet to mitigate any confusion. It is also very important that your full name and address be clearly noted on each CD, DVD, print, description and thumbnail page submitted.

CLOSING THOUGHTS

As integral as your portfolio is for gaining acceptance and earning scholarships, it's more than just a pawn in the application process. Your portfolio is a window into who you are. Even a single idea within it reveals far more information than you'd think, offering

"Fruit Still-life" by Eunbi Lee, admitted to Parsons with a $104,000 scholarship award.

insight into your thought process in the moment of creation, the environment you came from, and the direction in which you're heading.

Contrary to popular belief, ideas do not come from some magical source of creativity within, but from a synthesis of your experiences. Through artistic training, you learn to express these ideas with skill and proficiency. The more time you invest in practicing technique, the more refined your expressions will be. And those individuals who can express their ideas with clarity, purpose, and honesty are the ones who can craft genuine, authentic, original portfolios that win scholarship awards and gain them admission to the world's most highly-ranked undergraduate programs.

"The Keeper of Time" by Erica Byun, admitted to Cornell University with a $206,000 scholarship.

1

THE COOPER UNION

> " THE COOPER UNION IS ONE OF VERY FEW AMERICAN INSTITUTIONS OF HIGHER LEARNING THAT OFFERS A FULL TUITION SCHOLARSHIP TO EVERY ADMITTED STUDENT."

1

THE COOPER UNION

In the U.S. there is a privately funded college known as the Cooper Union, which grants full scholarships to all of its students. It is located in the East Village neighborhood of Manhattan and was founded in 1859 by Peter Cooper, the inventor and philanthropist who designed the first steam locomotive in the U.S.

Cooper Union's 41 Cooper Square, completed in Summer 2009, was primarily designed to house their School of Engineering and School of Art.

For 152 years Cooper Union has been a leading college for art and architecture within the nation. So it comes as no surprise that it's widely perceived as one of the most challenging colleges to acquire admission to in the United States. In fact, if an admitted student demonstrates the need, the school will even cover a student's housing expenses for an entire academic year.

The Cooper Union itself comprises three main schools: the Albert Nerkin School of Engineering, the Irwin S. Chanin School of Architecture, and the School of Art. Only the Schools of Architecture and Art require students to complete home tests to gain admission.

The School of Architecture offers a 5-year Bachelor of Architecture program and a 2-year Master of Architecture II program. The School of Art offers a 4-year Bachelor of Fine Art program. Students looking to major in art end up graduating from Cooper Union with degrees in Studio Art, but are free to choose courses in Painting, Drawing, Photography, Printmaking, Sculpture, Film/Video, and Graphic Design until graduation.

Students in the School of Architecture, as freshmen, take courses in Architecture Studio, Architecture History, Techniques, Freehand Drawing, and Descriptive Geometry/CAD. Students in the School of Art, as freshmen, are required to take Basic Drawing, 2-D Design, 3-D Design, Color Theory, Technique, and Art History.

The approximate number of students

One of several "fishbowl" classrooms in 41 Cooper Square that feature prevalent floor-to-ceiling glass walls.

enrolled in the School of Architecture and the School of Art at any given time is always 250 and 550 respectively. And each year, only 35 students are admitted to the School of Architecture program and only 65 students are admitted to the School of Art.

The Cooper Union was built on the founding fundamental belief that an education "equal to the best" should be accessible to those who qualify, independent of their race, religion, sex, wealth or social status. Its popularity remains at an all-time high for its long-established reputation and the promising benefits of a tuition-free, yet first-class, education; art students from around the world, especially in Europe and Asia, aspire to attain admission and, every year, the competition is fierce: the School of Architecture accepts only 4.3% of its applicants whereas the School of Art accepts only 5% of its applicants each year. The main reasons for the recent rise in the number of applicants can be attributed to the annually increasing costs of college, global economic downturns, and the growth of education industries in emerging nations around the world.

"Bleed, Blister, and Purge" by Lisa Nikaido, admitted to Cooper Union's School of Art.

Notable Cooper Union alums include Thomas Edison; Kevin Burke, CEO of Con Edison; Daniel Libeskind, architect of the Jewish Museum in Berlin; Russell Hulse, winner of the 1993 Nobel Prize in Physics; and Bob Kane, the comic book artist credited for creating Batman.

ART REQUIREMENTS FOR COOPER UNION SCHOOL OF ART APPLICANTS

At the time of this writing, all applicants should submit:

① A portfolio of 15-20 artworks in slide format – be sure to include many pieces that have elements that are drawn from observation;

② Five artworks in their original state – if you're accepted, you'll get these back within 2 years, if you're rejected, you'll get these back within 6 months;
③ Your home test solutions; and
④ Your sketchbook (not required, but strongly recommended).

In the end, everything must fit into the 13" x 17" envelope provided to you by the school. Make sure you all drawings are fixed prior to mailing. Do not rip or tape the envelope.

COOPER UNION'S HOME TEST
Though Cooper Union changes its home test questions every year, as an applicant to their School of Architecture, you can expect to visually solve nine problems presented on 9 separate sheets of 11" x 14" paper. How creatively you use composition, dimensionality, perspective, and visual perception in your solutions will serve as determining factors for an admissions decision by the school. In addition to these 9 problems, you will also have to answer a series of questions in writing.

As an applicant to their School of Art, you can expect to be presented with six (very conceptual) questions to which

Discussions drive the majority of non-studio courses in the Cooper Union's School of Art. Many of these courses are held in classrooms that are devoid of fixed furniture to allow for more modular and versatile uses of space.

"The Labyrinth" by Jennifer Kim, admitted to Cooper Union's School of Architecture.

you must create visual solutions. The questions are designed by the school to measure your creative potential.

CLOSING THOUGHTS

Once you have sent out your application, Cooper Union will mail you a copy of their home test in about 3-4 weeks. Once you receive it, you will be given only about another 3-4 weeks to complete it. Keep this time frame in mind when you are brainstorming solutions. Also it'll prove important for you to understand that beyond technique, the Cooper Union looks for students whose home test solutions are thematically cohesive and conceptually unique.

APPLICATION DEADLINES

EARLY DECISION DEADLINE

December 2

41 Cooper Square features a full-height Grand Atrium, which reduces energy costs by allowing more natural light. In fact, in 2010, 41 Cooper Square became the first academic and laboratory structure in New York City to meet Platinum-level LEED standards for energy efficiency.

REGULAR DECISION DEADLINES

January 9 for School of Art applicants

January 6 for School of Architecture applicants

ADMISSIONS OFFICE

The Cooper Union
Admissions Department
30 Cooper Square, Third Floor
New York, NY 10003-7120

RHODE ISLAND SCHOOL OF DESIGN

> " RISD OFFERS HYBRIDIZED COURSES IN BUSINESS & DESIGN WITH MIT WHERE RISD STUDENTS COLLABORATE WITH STUDENTS FROM MIT'S SLOAN SCHOOL OF BUSINESS TO DISCUSS THE VIABILITY, MARKETABILITY, AND PROFITABILITY OF PRODUCTS DESIGNED BY RISD STUDENTS. "

2

RHODE ISLAND SCHOOL OF DESIGN

RISD was established in Providence, Rhode Island (the smallest US state), in 1877. The school enrolls 1,920 undergraduates in 16 undergraduate programs and 370 graduates in 17 graduate programs annually.

RISD WANTS ITS STUDENTS TO DEVELOP RANGE

On May 13th, 2009, President Obama stressed the importance of an "integrated education" during a commencement speech at Arizona State University. The idea stressed the importance of future college graduates to be equipped with a broad range of knowledge, skills, and work experience to thrive in today's job market.

College Hill in Providence, Rhode Island, refers to the two major educational institutions established in the neighborhood: Rhode Island School of Design and Brown University.

To develop range, students must be exposed to more. This could very well be why RISD offers hybridized courses in Business & Design with MIT where RISD students collaborate with students from MIT's Sloan School of Business to discuss the viability, marketability, and profitability of products designed by RISD students. Every facet of the design process is considered jointly: innovation, manufacturing, distribution, marketing, budgeting, timeframes, and deliverables. As a result, these projects lead to learning experiences that are far more encompassing, immersive, and empowering. Graduates of these courses can go on to effect real change in small businesses, local communities and beyond.

What also sets RISD apart from other art colleges is the fact that it receives excellent sponsorship from companies and organizations (think Microsoft and NASA) which in turn provide its students with an array of distinct joint programs year-after-year.

Moreover, RISD is the only art college in the US that offers a joint dual-degree

The RISD Museum, founded in 1877, houses over 86,000 works by prominent international and American artists – including Picasso, Monet, Manet, and Andy Warhol – and serves as an invaluable resource for RISD's students.

RISD is the only art college in the U.S. to offer a joint dual-degree program with an Ivy League University: Brown.

Each spring a jury of professionals in the field visits RISD to select the best student-made apparel for a popular runway show.

program with an Ivy League college: Brown. Students who are admitted to this extremely competitive and intensive program are afforded the opportunity to earn two undergraduate degrees, one from each college, in 5 years.

In order to gain admission to this specialized dual-degree program, otherwise known as the Brown+RISD dual-degree program, applicants must first follow each school's individual application instructions, gain admission to both schools separately, then complete supplementary requirements in order to be eligible for a final review by a joint Brown+RISD admissions committee; applicants are then notified of a final admissions decision in early March.

Did you know? Only 13-15 students are admitted to the Brown + RISD dual-degree program each year, making it one of the most difficult undergraduate programs to gain admission to in the world.

RISD also provides its single-degree students with the exclusive opportunity to take courses at Brown, whose campus is adjacent to that of

RISD's, to earn college credits and receive a farther-reaching educational experience.

Additionally, RISD's expansive campus and the state-of-the-art facilities allow its students to take courses in Pottery, Visual Arts, Film, Animation, Video, Fashion, Architecture Design, Graphic Design, Product Design, Printmaking, Painting, Interior, Architecture, Sculpture, Metal Works, Industrial Design, Illustration, Photography, Textiles, Glass Arts & Crafts, and Jewelry Design.

"Bicycle Home Test" by Heewon Yang, admitted to RISD with a $70,400 scholarship award.

RISD'S PORTFOLIO SUBMISSION GUIDELINES

RISD will also require you to reproduce and submit 2-3 pages from your journal or sketchbook to indicate your process of research, thinking and investigation.

RISD'S HOME TEST

As of 2012, RISD's home test requires two drawings. Your first drawing must reference a bicycle. Your second drawing should be chosen from this list of options:

① In the course of a single calendar day, draw 25 related images in a single visualization

② Visualize the invisible

③ A drawing that uses both sides of the sheet of paper

④ An image of water, from an observed body of water. It should include the following: something visible from the bottom, something floating under the surface, something alive, things floating on the surface, the reflection of sky, the reflection of something terrestrial, water surface patterns or rhythms (from wind), light on the surface of the water, light coming from underneath the water, and hierarchy (both tiny to large and crowded to open).

Each drawing must be done on a sheet of white paper measuring 16" x 20" (40 cm x 50 cm). Your bicycle drawing must be done using graphite pencil. For your second drawing sample, you may use graphite pencil or any dry (fixable) medium, a water-based medium (such as acrylic, ink, watercolor or gouache) or a combination of these media. Do not, however, use any oil-based medium, or collage, for your second drawing and remember that whatever medium(s) you choose for this drawing, you must be able to fold your solution and mail it to RISD's office.

You may approach these two drawings in any way you wish. For example, your drawings may be abstract expressions or representational observations; you may choose to draw an object alone or place it in a situation; you may choose to cover the entire surface of the page or only a small portion of it, etc. Other than the stated requirements related to paper size (16" x 20"), subject (i.e., bicycle) and medium (graphite pencil),

"The Answers" by Areen Kim, admitted to RISD as a transfer student with a $120,000 scholarship award.

everything and anything else are up to you.

These drawings must be submitted in their original form, not as reproductions. When you're done, fold your drawings in half and then in half again to a finished size of 8" x 10" (20cm x 25cm) and be sure to note your full name and address on the back of each drawing.

FOCUS ON PROCESS

Drawing is as much about process as presentation, so I encourage you to consider your drawing submissions as exercises in experimental thinking and risk-taking more than final presentations or examples of technical proficiency. Consider the full range of possible expression in your submissions, as RISD may not value any particular style of drawing more than another. Finally, using photographs as a source for your drawings is not recommended.

RISD'S WRITING SAMPLES

Submit two examples of writing, each between 200 and 400 words. Your first sample should address, "What is the most important thing you hope will have happened to you as a result of your time in the RISD community?"

Your second sample should be chosen from this list of options:

① Every day we're confronted by circumstances that range from the worrisome to the inspiring. What do

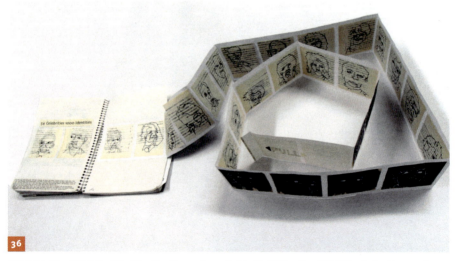

"54 Celebrities, 1000 Identities" by Alex Khomyakov, admitted to RISD with a $92,000 scholarship award.

RISD requires applicants to reproduce and submit 2-3 pages from their journals or sketchbooks to indicate their processes of research, thinking and investigation.

you find most compelling in the world right now? How might this impact our future? What influence can you have on this situation?

② Create a short piece of fiction, in the form of a story, essay, poem or other genre.

③ Is there something you love, have to do, can't stop thinking about? Write about a personal passion or obsession other than visual art or design.

④ A rubber ball, two inches in diameter. Make a list of 50 things you could do with this ball. OK, let's be reasonable, 25 would be good. OK, final offer, make a list of things, length of the list up to you... and the length of the list is not the most important thing, is it?

It should be noted that RISD awards fewer scholarships than other art colleges. In order to win a scholarship award from RISD, you must possess a solid GPA, high test scores, a strong art portfolio and unique home test solutions. Simply put, you must demonstrate to RISD that you have the potential for growth and that you, from the school's standpoint, are worth investing in.

Fact! *RISD's tuition costs have risen from $36,371 to $38,295 (a 4.9% increase) since 2009.*

APPLICATION DEADLINES

EARLY DECISION DEADLINE

December 15

REGULAR DECISION DEADLINE

February 1

Tip! *RISD's application deadlines aren't postmark dates; all of your required credentials must be in their office by the deadline.*

ADMISSIONS OFFICE

Admissions Office
Rhode Island School of Design
2 College Street, Providence,
Rhode Island 02903

3

CORNELL UNIVERSITY

> " ONE DISTINCT ADVANTAGE OF CORNELL'S ART PROGRAM IS THAT IT ENABLES AMBITIOUS UNDERGRADUATES TO PURSUE PROGRAMS OF STUDY IN TWO COLLEGES AND EARN BOTH A B.F.A. DEGREE AND A B.A. DEGREE FROM THE UNIVERSITY."

CORNELL UNIVERSITY

Cornell University, located in Ithaca, New York, was founded in 1865 and started the country's first colleges for hotel administration, industrial and labor relations, and veterinary medicine. Cornell now offers a wide variety of undergraduate programs and runs interdisciplinary research centers for nanotechnology, supercomputing, and more.

Cornell is often perceived to be the easiest Ivy to gain admission to. However, when this claim is examined more closely, one finds that Cornell enrolls three-to-four times more undergraduate freshmen per year than other Ivies, but the school does not subscribe to academic standards that are any lower.

Cornell's main campus is on East Hill in Ithaca, New York, and sprawls across roughly 745 acres of land.

A panoramic shot of Cornell's Central Campus covered in snow.

Fact! Cornell is a private university, a land-grant institution of New York State, and the most educationally diverse member in the Ivy League.

Although Cornell is a private university, it also receives financial support from New York State. As a result, tuition costs for students whose families are residents of New York are much cheaper ($21,814/year) than for out-of-state students ($37,954/year).

To aid students from low-income families, Cornell also partnered with New York's Educational Opportunity Program (EOP) and Higher Education Opportunity Program (HEOP) to grant qualifying students full four-year tuition scholarships.

Fact! Cornell even grants scholarship awards to its international students who make up nearly 9% of its undergraduate student body.

Cornell University comprises 11 colleges including its art college, The College of Architecture, Art, and Planning. Students admitted into Cornell's Undergraduate Studio Art Degree Program found within its College of Architecture, Art, and Planning are offered 6 major areas of coursework to choose from:

① **COMBINED MEDIA**
Includes coursework in Film, Video, Stage, Dance, Music and Textile Design, and Fashion Design;

② **ELECTRONIC IMAGING**
Includes coursework in Digital Imaging, Video, Animation;

③ **PAINTING**;

④ **PHOTOGRAPHY**;

⑤ **PRINTMAKING**; and

⑥ **SCULPTURE**.

"Beyond Reality" by Erica Byun, admitted to Cornell with a $206,000 scholarship.

"Summer's Storm" by Kelly Lee, admitted early to Cornell's Art Program.

BECOME MORE OPEN, ADAPTIVE, AND CREATIVE

One distinct advantage of Cornell's Art Program is that it enables ambitious undergraduates to pursue programs of study in two colleges and earn both a B.F.A. degree from Cornell's College of Art, Architecture, and Planning and a Bachelor of Arts degree from Cornell's College of Arts and Sciences, College of Human Ecology, or College of Engineering. Combining coursework across college boundaries can enlarge the scope of a student's undergraduate experience and help her become more open, adaptive, and creative.

Fact! Earning two degrees usually requires 10 semesters; the university provides eligible students with financial aid for the entire period.

Remember to carefully review the information online on the college in Cornell to which you're applying. Having researched your intended college(s) will prove greatly advantageous when the time comes to write your college interest essay on the Cornell Supplement.

ARCHITECTURE MAJORS: DON'T OVERLOOK NAAB-ACCREDITATION

In choosing a college for architecture,

make sure that you'll be earning a professional degree accredited by the National Architectural Accrediting Board (NAAB). If the degree you're working towards is not accredited by the NAAB, even after completing a 5-year architecture program, you may still be required to complete separate coursework at another college that is NAAB-accredited in order to receive an architect's license. For example, Stanford University's Architectural Engineering Program offers NAAB-accreditation whereas Cornell University's Architectural Design Program awards architecture and planning design certificates to all of its graduates who have completed 180 credits.

The Department of City and Regional Planning offers coursework in Architectural Planning, Architectural Theory, History of Architecture Design, Environmental Design, and Landscape Design. Students may also choose to complete this coursework at either Cornell's Ithaca or Manhattan campus – more direct (and practical) field training is available at Cornell's Manhattan campus.

"Public Art Concept Design" by Grace Ma, admitted to Cornell's City and Regional Planning Program.

"The Wages of Sin" by Timothy Lee, admitted to Cornell University's Dual B.F.A Studio Art and B.A. Neuroscience Program.

"Doors of Perception" by Stella Chung, admitted to Cornell with a $39,100 scholarship award.

Tip! Give yourself enough time before the application deadline to complete both the Common Application and the Cornell Supplement.

At the time of this writing, the average scores of admitted freshmen are as follows:

SAT CRITICAL READING: 67% scored 650 or above.
SAT MATH: 82% scored 650 or above.
CLASS RANK: 88% ranked in the top 10% of their class.

Fact! Cornell requires all Architecture and Art applicants to have completed either ① three years of one foreign language; or ② two foreign languages, two years each.

Students at Cornell may also change their majors after beginning coursework in a particular program if it is not to their liking via Cornell's Office of Internal Transfer. At Cornell, there are two types of internal transfer between colleges:

DIRECT TRANSFER

Through Cornell's Direct Transfer Program, it's possible to be admitted directly into a new program. To be eligible for direct transfer, you usually have to be taking, or have successfully completed, courses in your proposed major. Some colleges require that students take major courses the semester immediately prior to the intended transfer. If you are uncertain if you immediately qualify for direct transfer, you can contact their office.

CONDITIONAL TRANSFER

Students, who do not meet the criteria for direct transfer, may be considered for conditional transfer. Generally, students whose current curriculum differs substantially from their target college, or students with a below average academic record, are considered for conditional transfer. Conditional transfer guarantees admission the following semester, if you successfully complete the conditional transfer requirements set by the target college. During the conditional transfer semester, students pay the tuition and fees of their target college.

Tip! *Architecture & Art applicants should schedule face-to-face interviews to present their work in person.*

APPLICATION DEADLINES

EARLY ACTION DEADLINE
November 1
REGULAR DECISION DEADLINE
January 2

ADMISSIONS OFFICE

Office of Undergraduate Admissions
College of Architecture, Art, and Planning
Cornell University
235 Sibley Dome
Ithaca, NY 14853-6701

PRATT INSTITUTE

> " PRATT, WHICH WAS FOUNDED IN 1887, IS ONE OF THE FEW ART COLLEGES IN NEW YORK CITY THAT OFFERS STUDENTS A FULL CAMPUS EXPERIENCE. "

PRATT INSTITUTE

Near the end of the 20th century, as property became more and more expensive in Manhattan, many gallerists and artists began looking for more affordable studio and gallery space towards an area of Brooklyn known as Dumbo (or Down Under the Manhattan Bridge Overpass). Through gentrification, many abandoned and dilapidated factory buildings in Dumbo have been converted over the years into upscale restaurants, chic storefronts, and luxury condominiums. Perhaps this is why a large and prestigious art college within close proximity to Dumbo (a five-minute drive) has gained so much popularity in communities of art and education in recent years as one of

Pratt's Sculpture Park is the largest sculpture garden in New York City and has featured sculptures by artists such as Richard Serra, Donald Lipski, and Mark di Suvero.

the best choices for emerging creative types in the Northeast: Pratt Institute.

Pratt, which was founded in 1887, is one of the few art colleges in New York City that offers students a full campus experience. Its campus sprawls across 25 acres in the Clinton Hill area of Brooklyn and is just a metro ride away from Manhattan. The campus is filled with historic buildings and offers students a library and an athletic center among other amenities.

Did you know? *Notable Pratt alumni include Felix Gonzalez Torres, Eva Hesse, Ellsworth Kelly, Max Weber, Betsey Johnson, Joshua Davis, and Paul Rand.*

In order to attract outstanding applicants, Pratt awards a great number of scholarship awards to incoming undergraduate freshmen every year. In fact, a whopping 60% of admitted freshmen attend Pratt on scholarship awards.

Moreover, applicants with creative portfolios, high marks in school, and above-average test scores have exceedingly high chances of winning full-tuition scholarships from Pratt. The school even awards scholarships ranging from $3,000 to $10,000 to its international students.

Another benefit of applying to Pratt

In 2010, fashion majors at Pratt created inventive, wearable paper sculptures that were displayed on Ralph Pucci mannequins in the storefront windows of Macy's Herald Square, the largest department store in the US.

The Pratt Sculpture Park was recognized as one of the 10 best college and university campus art collections in the country by Public Art Review in 2006.

Pratt's campus stretches across 25 acres; features historic buildings, a library, and an athletic center; and is a short walk of two blocks from the Clinton-Washington Avenues subway station.

is that all undergraduate first-year applicants are automatically considered for scholarship awards – additional scholarship essays or supplemental materials are not required.

Talented students from low-income backgrounds may also qualify for full scholarships from the Higher Education Opportunity Program, or **HEOP**. Eligibility depends on the number of family members in your household and your family's annual income. At the time of this writing, the application deadline for **HEOP** in New York City is February 1. More information is available at *www.heop.org*.

Furthermore, every student who has won a National Portfolio Gold or National Portfolio Silver Key Award from the Scholastic Art & Writing Award Competition (www.artandwriting.org) are automatically awarded $1,500 and $1,000 scholarship awards respectively by Pratt upon admission.

PRATT'S TOP PROGRAMS

Interior Design, Architecture, and Product Design are some of the most popular and competitive programs at Pratt. In fact, U.S. News & World Report ranked Pratt's Interior Design program #1 in the U.S. in 2009. Also, Pratt's Product Design program has ranked as

...+ in the U.S. in the past and its ...aphic Design program has ranked as high as #9 in the U.S.

Tip! *At the time of this writing, Pratt requires applicants to specify primary and secondary fields of study they are interested in on their application. Although, applicants may mark their primary field of study as "Undecided" (statistically 15% of all applicants choose this option) they must declare a specific major of interest for their secondary field of study. It is wise to be honest with your selections during this part of the application as many of Pratt's highly ranked programs can prove to be difficult to transfer into as a non-freshman later on.*

PRATT'S SCHOOLS

Pratt is separated into four main schools: the School of Architecture, the School of Liberal Arts and Sciences, the School of Art & Design, and the School of Information and Library Sciences. Through each of these schools, students can earn undergraduate degrees in Animation, Advertisement, Art and Design Education, Art History and Theory, Fashion Design, Film/Video, Graphic Design, Industrial Design, Interior Design, Jewelry, Photography, Illustration, Painting, Printmaking, Sculpture, Theory & Criticism, Art History, Design, and Architecture.

Many of the aforementioned majors break down into more specialized fields. For example, the School of Architecture offers concentrations in General Architecture, Construction Management, and Building and

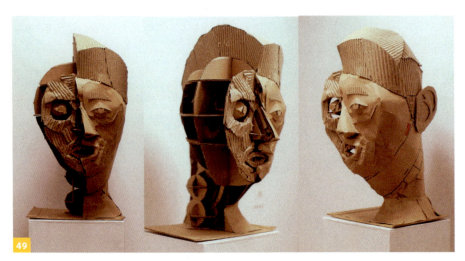

"Cubist Head" by Eric Mun, admitted to Pratt with a $125,000 scholarship award.

"Reversal of Nature" by Matt Kim, admitted to Pratt with a $100,000 scholarship award.

"The Immortal Embrace" by Julia Wollner, admitted to Pratt with a $15,000 scholarship.

Construction Management; within the School of Design, students can choose to concentrate their coursework in Package Design, Web Design, and Motion Design classes; and in the School of Education, students may concentrate coursework in Art and Design Education, Art Therapy/Creative Development, and Art Therapy.

As for Associate Degree programs, Pratt offers students a concise, comprehensive, and intensive 2-year Associates Degree Program, which grants its graduates A.O.S. degrees; and an Associates of Applied Science Degree Program, which grants its graduates A.A.S. degrees. Both programs operate out of Pratt's Manhattan campus located on 14th Street between 6th and 7th Avenues. The A.A.S. program is particular in that graduates of this program can opt to transfer into third-year programs to ultimately graduate from Pratt with four-year Bachelors of Art degrees in Painting, Graphic Design, Illustration, or Building and Construction. The A.O.S. program on the other hand, does not allow this, and all A.O.S. degree students graduate with Associate Degrees in Graphic Design, Illustration, or Digital Design & Interactive Media. Pratt offers 18 graduate programs: Architecture, Architecture and Urban Design, City & Regional Planning, Facilities Management, Historic Preservation, Urban Environmental Systems Management, Art and Design Education, Art Therapy and Creativity Development, Communications Design, Digital Arts, Dance/Movement Therapy, Design Management, Fine Arts, Industrial Design, Interior Design, Package Design, Museum Studies, and Theory and Criticism.

Students in Pratt's Industrial Design graduate program can choose to concentrate their courses in Transportation Design, Electronic Product Design, Lighting Design, Vessel Design, or Furniture Design.

What is also unique to Pratt is its Writing and Tutorial Center, or WTC, which tutors students in Art History, Math, Physics, Statics, Steel, Writing, and Conversational Speaking for free. This center should be taken full advantage of by every student at Pratt who is looking to improve her writing skills.

PRATT WANTS YOU TO GET A HEAD START ON YOUR CAREER

Pratt also sets up opportunities for its students to visit the offices of major design companies in New York City. These visits serve to inform students of the skill sets they'll need to develop in order to land an art-related job in New York City. Such experiences can embolden students in their final undergraduate years and grant them the additional drive needed to outmatch

National-award winning "Boots of Travel" by Heewon Yang, admitted to Pratt with a $61,000 scholarship award.

their peers.

Internship fairs are also held twice a year at Pratt for its third and fourth-year undergraduates. These fairs are great opportunities for students to learn about a variety of job opportunities and introduce themselves to prospective employers. What's more, Pratt's Manhattan Campus offers a gallery space where students with outstanding work can more effectively showcase and promote their skills.

All seniors in B.F.A. degree programs at Pratt, however, can get a head start on their careers through the school's Senior Shows as representatives from large corporations, agencies, and galleries often attend such openings to recruit, interview, or create write-ups on young emerging talent.

"The Perpetual Shedding of One's Ignorance" by Hannah Sung, admitted to Pratt with a $60,000 scholarship award.

ADMISSIONS OFFICE
Pratt Institute
Office of Admissions
200 Willoughby Avenue
Brooklyn, NY 11205

APPLICATION DEADLINES

EARLY ACTION DEADLINE
November 1
REGULAR DECISION DEADLINE
January 5

5

PARSONS
THE NEW SCHOOL FOR DESIGN

> " GRADUATES OF PARSONS' FASHION PROGRAM LEAVE PREPARED TO ENTER THE FASHION INDUSTRY IN AREAS SUCH AS FASHION, COSTUME AND ACCESSORY DESIGN, MARKETING, MERCHANDISING, CURATORIAL WORK, AND INTERIOR DESIGN. "

5

PARSONS
THE NEW SCHOOL FOR DESIGN

Parsons The New School For Design, or better known as Parsons, is the art and design college of The New School University and was founded in 1896. It is located in New York City's Greenwich Village, and has produced artists and designers such as Marc Jacobs, Dean and Dan Caten, Norman Rockwell, Donna Karan, Jane Frank, William Gropper, Tom Ford and Tom Morrow. Like most universities in New York City, Parsons's campus is spread throughout the city, but its main building is located at 13th Street and 5th Avenue.

Parsons offers twenty-five different undergraduate and graduate programs each housed in one of five schools:

Since its founding, Parsons The New School for Design has made efforts to bridge art and design by creating programs that actively relate and converse with one another within Parsons' multiple-school structure and within its wider New School network.

① School of Art and Design History and Theory
② School of Art, Media, and Technology
③ School of Constructed Environments
④ School of Design Strategies: Cities, Services, Ecosystems
⑤ School of Fashion

At the time of this writing, Parsons has almost 3,800 undergraduate and 400 graduate students and offers exchange programs with other eminent art schools from around the world including Parsons Paris School of Art and Design in France, the Kanazawa International Design Institute in Japan, and La Escuela de Diseño at Altos de Chavón in the Dominican Republic.

In the summer of 2010, thirty one-of-a-kind works of art and fashion "walked" down Broadway during the temporary installation of Sidewalk Catwalk, which included designs by Parsons students. The public art display attracted art devotees and fashionistas alike.

MUCH MORE THAN JUST FASHION

Parsons offers BFA degrees in Architectural Design, Communication Design, Design and Technology, Environmental Studies, Fashion Design, Fine Arts, Illustration, Integrated Design, Interior Design, Photography, and Product Design.

Parsons also offers Bachelor of Business Administration (B.B.A.) degrees through its Design and Management Program, Bachelor of Science (B.S.) degrees through its Urban Design Program, and combined Bachelor of Arts and Bachelor of Science (B.A/B.S.) degrees in Environmental Studies.

For the professional prepared to make the leap into design, Parsons offers Associate in Applied Science (A.A.S.) degrees in Fashion Design, Fashion Marketing, Graphic Design, and Interior Design.

Did you know? *Parsons's Integrated Design Program (B.F.A.) prepares students to enter a*

A team of Parsons students competing to take the top spot in a week-long conceptual art and design competition involving the refashioning of thousands of dollars worth of Louis Vuitton fabric samples for a chance to achieve international recognition.

variety of design careers or pursue advanced design study. Many graduates even combine design with entrepreneurship by starting innovative design businesses.

FIRST-YEAR OPTIONS AT PARSONS

Parsons offers students flexibility in choosing paths of study. As a freshman, students can begin their undergraduate studies in Parsons' Foundation program, which offers a broad introduction to tools that are applicable to any creative endeavor. Or, if students are interested in one of the following majors, they can enter a special first-year track that lets them begin studies in their field right away: Design and Management, Design and Technology, Environmental Studies, Photography, and Urban Design. Students can switch majors in their sophomore year after an academic review, regardless of what they choose as their first-year program.

Parsons vs FIT: *All students admitted to FIT's work towards 2-year associate (AAS) degrees whereas all students admitted to Parsons work towards 4-year bachelor (BFA) degrees. All FIT students who end their AAS courses with a cumulative GPA above a "B," however, qualify to move on to complete an additional 2 years of coursework at FIT to earn a bachelor's (BFA) degree.*

A FOUNDATION IN DESIGN

Upon completion of Parsons's first-year Foundation program, Fashion Design students begin an intensive sophomore year by concentrating on garment construction. They study sewing, draping, and patternmaking, as well as drawing and digital design. An emphasis on design concepts during these years complements students' technical skills and provides them with an overview of fashion design markets.

Did you know? The majority of Parsons Fashion majors spend their foundation year taking liberal arts classes and studio art classes in Parson's main building located at 13th Street and 5th Avenue. Starting sophomore year, students take courses concentrated in fashion in buildings scattered throughout New York's Garment District.

STRENGTH IN DESIGN

Through courses in business, fashion history, and digital design, students broaden their knowledge and vocabulary and begin to refine their design work in both concept and execution. Design Concepts, taken in the sophomore year, introduces students to merchandising, fabrication, trend analysis, and other parameters that clarify the message of a collection. Students find their voices as designers and identify the audiences they will cultivate as professionals through coursework; competitions; a junior-year partnership with the Gap, Inc.; and the development of a three-look collection.

BUILDING A COLLECTION

Senior year is devoted almost entirely to the thesis project. Students develop three-collection concepts, one of which is selected for completion and presented to a jury of industry professionals. In conjunction with the thesis project, students develop a portfolio and participate in several high-level competitions. Collections are documented and presented in Parsons' online Look Book.

POISED FOR SUCCESS

Graduates of Parsons' Fashion

Self-portrait by Crystal Norbert, admitted to Parsons with a $104,000 scholarship award.

Program leave prepared to enter the fashion industry in areas such as fashion, costume and accessory design, marketing, merchandising, curatorial work, and interior design.

PARSONS VS. FIT: DID YOU KNOW?
Parsons looks for portfolio pieces and home test solutions that are more fine art based than the Fashion Institute of Technology, which looks for work that is more fashion-focused.

LEARN ABOUT THE BUSINESS OF FASHION WITH COLUMBIA UNIVERSITY STUDENTS
Through Parson's partnership with the Luxury Education Foundation, Parsons has, for the past 15 years, enabled its students to collaborate with MBA students from Columbia University to develop brand-strengthening design solutions for luxury companies that, in the past, have included Cartier, Christian Dior, Hermès, Lalique, Louis Vuitton, and Luxottica.

This program allows students to meet at Parsons, Columbia University, and the offices of the companies' chief executives for discussion and working sessions. In the past, student projects have focused on a range of topics including product innovation, corporate branding, and the marketing tactics required to sell a luxury experience.

Recent projects through this program have included a next-generation retail experience for Cartier; a luxury service program for Christian Dior; a marketing campaign for the launch of Hermès first online men's boutique; an integrated marketing campaign that included limited-edition packaging designs for the 150th anniversary of Lalique; a new branding strategy for Louis Vuitton accessories; and marketing strategies for Ralph Lauren Purple Label Eyewear.

"Foes" by Hannah Kim, admitted to Parsons with a full-tuition scholarship award.

WHAT INTERNSHIP OPPORTUNITIES DOES PARSONS OFFER?

Many undergraduate departments include a professional internship as part of the degree requirements. Some also grant credit for internships that students obtain independently or through the Office of Career Services. Parsons students have interned at Marc Jacobs, Polo-Ralph Lauren, HBO, MTV, the New York Times, Rolling Stone magazine, Marvel Comics, the Museum of Modern Art, among many other companies and institutions.

Did you know? The New School is currently constructing its first ever University Center on 14th Street. When the construction is complete, the University Center will offer state-of-the-art facilities, including fully wired "smart" classrooms, design studios, a student residence, and an auditorium with a convertible runway.

THE PARSONS CHALLENGE

All BFA, BBA, BA/BFA, and BS applicants are required to complete the Parsons Challenge and submit it to Parsons via SlideRoom only. CDs,

"Bedroom in Brooklyn" by Kateryna Murygina, admitted to Parsons as a transfer student.

DVDs, slides, original artwork, power point presentations, binders, and flash drives are not accepted.

The Challenge: Explore something usually overlooked within your daily environment. Choose one object, location, or activity. Using any medium or media, interpret your discovery in 3 original pieces. Support each piece of art with an essay of approximately 250 words.

The series should convey a conceptual and creative response of the subject matter you have chosen to discover. Parsons allows you to express your series in any medium: drawing, video, photography, sculpture, 3D work, collage, digital images, etc. You may choose to express your solution in one medium or many.

Your response to the Parsons Challenge helps Parsons' admissions committee better understand how you develop concepts and how you visually and verbally communicate your ideas.

Tip! *Applicants to Parsons' Design and Technology Program may include a sampling of their best digital pieces – digital collages,*

Fashion sketches done at Parsons by Angela Lee, admitted to Parsons with a $96,000 scholarship.

graphic design, web design, film, photography, or video – to enhance their candidacy for admission into this program.

APPLICATION DEADLINES

EARLY ACTION DEADLINE
November 1

REGULAR DECISION DEADLINE
February 1

ADMISSIONS OFFICE
Parsons The New School for Design
Office of Admission
72 Fifth Avenue
New York, NY 10011

6

THE SCHOOL OF VISUAL ARTS

> " SVA IS ONE OF THE FEW MANHATTAN BASED ART COLLEGES THAT PROVIDES ITS STUDENTS WITH COMPREHENSIVE COURSEWORK IN EMERGING ART FIELDS AND PROVIDES ENOUGH CAREER DEVELOPING RESOURCES TO LAND ITS GRADUATES JOBS. "

THE SCHOOL OF VISUAL ARTS

Many artists look to settle in New York City for its abundant resources and diverse cultural offerings. It is the city in which over 170 languages are spoken, over 150 museums operate, and over 2000 cultural organizations support and promote active artists on a daily basis.

As the most populous city in the US, the city New York exerts a significant impact upon global commerce, finance, media, fashion, research, technology, education, entertainment, and, of course, art. Because the city teems with working professionals engaged in a variety of occupations across all major industries, young creatives are faced with unparalleled opportunities to promote their skill sets and expand their professional networks.

SVA's main building, located at 209 East 23rd Street, features classrooms, administrative offices, a cafeteria (Moe's Cafe) and an amphitheater on the third floor. The upper floors are mostly designated for the film, video, graphic design, advertising, illustration and cartooning classes. The building's lobby and an adjoining room also serve as a museum space for exhibits and public events.

The School of Visual Arts, headquartered in the Gramercy Park area of Manhattan, is one of the few Manhattan based art colleges that provides its students with comprehensive coursework in emerging art fields and provides enough career developing resources to land its graduates jobs.

The School of Visual Arts, or SVA, was co-founded by Silas H. Rhodes and Burne Hogarth in 1947. It was first named the Cartoonists and Illustrators School and was renamed to the School of Visual Arts in 1956. To this day, SVA's Cartooning and Animation Programs are widely reputed as the best on the East Coast, while the cartooning and animation programs at the California Institute of the Arts (or CalArts), founded by Walt Disney in 1961, holds this title on the West Coast.

SVA offers over 2,300 courses each year. Over 3,300 students of 45 different nationalities make up its diverse undergraduate student body. The school offers undergraduate degrees in Animation, Cartooning, Computer Art, Film & Video, Fine Arts, Graphic Design, Illustration, Interior Design, Photography, etc. Graduate

SVA invites dealers and curators from around New York City to its biannual Open Studio events to provide its graduating students with opportunities to forge important connections.

"Surveillance" by Hiann Lee, admitted to SVA with a $60,000 scholarship award.

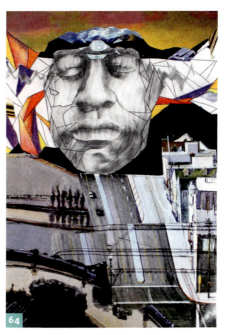

"A Mirror in the Roadway" by Joel Tschong, admitted to SVA with a $44,000 scholarship award.

degrees are offered in Photography, Video, Art Therapy, Art Education, Art Criticism, Computer Art, Graphic Design, Design Criticism, Fine Arts, and Interaction Design.

Fact! Notable SVA fine arts alumni include Sol Lewitt, a figurehead of the Conceptual Art movement and Keith Haring, a street artist and social activist whose work continues to inspire young artists in and around New York City today.

GRAPHIC DESIGNERS LOVE SVA

SVA's Graphic Design Program is also especially developed and offers its students comprehensive curriculums in three divisions of graphic design:

① **PRINT DESIGN**

Identity, books, editorials, posters, brochures, etc;

② **MOTION GRAPHICS**

Broadcast design, animated logos, video and film effects; and

③ **WEB DESIGN**

Dreamweaver CS5, Flash CS5, HTML5, CSS3, and jQuery.

SVA also offers state-of-the-art computer and printing facilities and offers courses taught by some of the industry's best: think Steven Heller, Joshua Davis, and Jason Santa Maria.

SVA WILL HELP YOU DEVELOP YOUR CAREER

SVA not only provides its students with comprehensive curriculums to develop specialized skill sets in the arts, but also a myriad of opportunities to gain real-world work experience within their specific fields of study to secure high-paying jobs upon graduation:

BIANNUAL NYC INTERNSHIP FAIRS

Every year, around October, various companies are selected by SVA to open booths at its bi-annual, winter and spring, internship fairs. Representatives from close to 700 companies and organizations participate in the fair each year. Companies that have attended the fair in the past include Marvel Comics, Nickelodeon, NBC, The Guggenheim Museum, Martha Stewart Living, MTV Networks, Sony BMG, Time Magazine, Pepsi, IKEA, FedEx, GE, BBDO, and many more. Students must have earned a GPA higher than 3.25 and have a portfolio of work in order to be eligible to attend.

Interviews are conducted at individual booths during the fair and hired students receive up to 150 hours of work experience and 3 college credits per semester. These fairs are great opportunities for any student looking

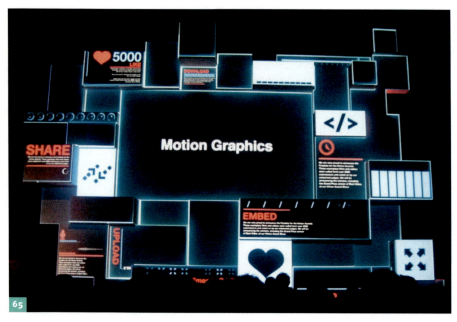

The School of Visual Arts Dusty Film & Animation Festival showcases the work of emerging filmmakers and animators from the Film, Video and Animation Department, launching many of them in their professional careers. More than 3,000 people attend the Dusty festival, which has garnered industry-wide recognition and is considered one of the top student film festivals in the country.

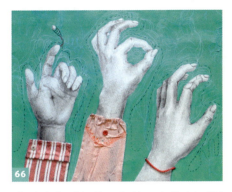

"Gesticulations" by Hannah Ahn, admitted to SVA with a $60,000 scholarship award.

"Self-portrait in Charcoal" by Angela Hyewon Kim, admitted to SVA's Honors Program.

to get a head start with her career in a ferociously competitive New York City job market. Don't miss out!

SENIOR SHOWS AT SVA

SVA also hosts Senior Shows every year for its students so that they may promote their work while simultaneously meeting a plethora of potential employers. The Senior Show for Motion Graphics majors, a specialized concentration found within SVA's graphic design program, is especially renowned as it takes place at Lincoln Center each year, where not only Pixar Animation Studios sends recruiters but also other top motion graphics, design and advertising agencies from around the world send recruiters as well.

DUSTY FILM AND ANIMATION FESTIVAL

Additionally, SVA also screens close to 100 short films by its graduating Film, Video and Animation majors each year at its 'Dusty Film and Animation Festival and Awards' show. The festival, which has taken place for more than 20 years now, provides its Film, Video and Animation graduates with unparalleled opportunities for recruitment by film directors, animation studios, and large film production houses.

In these ways and more, SVA prepares its students for successful careers through a range of effective career services that allow its students to promote and exhibit their work to large, relevant audiences.

APPLICATION DEADLINES

EARLY DECISION DEADLINE

December 1

PRIORITY DECISION DEADLINE

February 1 (Rolling)

ADMISSIONS OFFICE

School of Visual Arts

Office of Admissions

201 East 23 Street

New York, NY 10010-3994

7

CARNEGIE MELLON UNIVERSITY

" CMU IS WIDELY RECOGNIZED FOR ITS UNIQUE INTERDISCIPLINARY ENVIRONMENT, WHICH ENCOURAGES STUDENTS TO WORK ACROSS DEPARTMENTAL LINES. AS A RESULT, CMU'S GRADUATES ENTER THE WORLD WITH THE ABILITY TO SOLVE COMPLEX REAL-WORLD PROBLEMS. "

CARNEGIE MELLON UNIVERSITY

Carnegie Mellon University looks to "shape the world" through education, research and outreach. The school, which began as the Carnegie Technical Schools, was founded by the American steel magnate, Andrew Carnegie, in 1900. The school was renamed twice since: once in 1912 when it became the Carnegie Institute of Technology, and once again in 1967 when the Carnegie Institute of Technology merged with the Mellon Institute of Industrial Research to form what is now known as the Carnegie Mellon University, or CMU.

Fact! *Undergrads often work alongside professors who are leaders in their fields, with a student-faculty ratio of 10:1.*

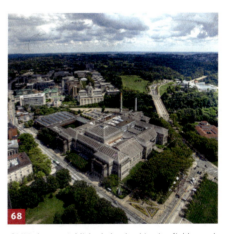

CMU has established leadership in fields such as computational finance, information systems management, arts management, product design, behavioral economics, human-computer interaction, entertainment technology, and decision science.

CMU's 140-acre campus offers students opportunities to engage in groundbreaking research. In fact, numerous Carnegie Mellon alumni have gone on to become Nobel Prize winners, tech company founders, inventors, orchestra conductors, Oscar-winning producers, and more.

Fact! Approximately 96 percent of faculty members have a Ph.D. or equivalent degree in their field. Ninety-nine percent of all undergraduate classes are taught by faculty, who often teach both undergraduate and graduate courses.

Carnegie Mellon University comprises seven colleges:

① **CARNEGIE INSTITUTE OF TECHNOLOGY**
College of Engineering

② **COLLEGE OF FINE ARTS**

③ **DIETRICH COLLEGE OF HUMANITIES AND SOCIAL SCIENCES**

④ **TEPPER SCHOOL OF BUSINESS**

⑤ **H. JOHN HEINZ III COLLEGE**
Public Policy & Information Systems

⑥ **MELLON COLLEGE OF SCIENCE**

⑦ **SCHOOL OF COMPUTER SCIENCE**

While students typically enroll in one of these seven schools, they still have the opportunity to study more than one discipline as CMU is widely recognized

Graduates of CMU's Entertainment Technology Center (ETC-Global) are among the most highly sought-after professionals in the interactive media industry.

for its unique interdisciplinary environment, which encourages students to work across departmental lines. As a result, CMU's graduates enter the world with the ability to solve complex real-world problems.

CROSS DISCIPLINES AT CMU FOR A RICHER EDUCATIONAL EXPERIENCE

The BXA, Intercollege Degree Programs, which comprises the Bachelor of Humanities & Arts (BHA) Program, the Bachelor of Science & Arts (BSA) Program, and the Bachelor of Computer Science & Arts (BCSA) Program, allows students the freedom to individualize their educational experience by "promoting integration, balance and innovation."

The letter X, the 24th letter of the alphabet, has always played an important part in mathematics and science. It is used as the symbol for an unknown or variable quantity. Similarly, in the bourgeoning field of interdisciplinary studies, the letter X symbolizes the quest for new forms of knowledge resulting from the mastery and fusion of multiple fields of inquiry. Carnegie Mellon University's BHA, BSA, and BCSA Intercollege Degree

70

In 2006, CMU installed Jonathan Borofsky's 100-foot-tall, seven-ton sculpture titled "Walking to the Sky" on its campus as a monument to human potential.

Programs have been conceived and developed on such premises.

The Bachelor of Humanities and Arts (BHA) Program began in 1993 as a response to numerous requests by Carnegie Mellon students to integrate studies in the fine arts with studies in the humanities or social sciences. The deans and faculty of the College of Fine Arts and the Dietrich College of Humanities and Social Sciences designed BHA as an innovative interdisciplinary degree-granting program that allows students the freedom to blend their interests between these two colleges.

The Bachelor of Science and Arts (BSA) Program was launched in 1999 as a joint venture between the College of Fine Arts and the Mellon College of Science. Based on the successful BHA model, the BSA curriculum is carefully designed to allow students the ability to balance studies in the fine arts with studies in the natural sciences or mathematics.

The Bachelor of Computer Science and Arts (BCSA) Program was created in 2008 by the College of Fine Arts and the School of Computer Science. It provides an ideal technical and conceptual foundation for students interested in pursuing fields which comprehensively meld technology and the arts such as game design, computer animation, computer music, interactive stagecraft, robotic art, and other emerging media.

Fact! *In order to gain admission to CMU's BXA Intercollege Degree Program, interested students must apply to and gain admission from both colleges within CMU.*

ART + TECHNOLOGY = FUTURE

As an aside, CMU's computer science program ranks as one of the best in the nation, rivaling even the undergraduate computer science programs found at MIT and Stanford. The school of computer science at CMU has even received financial backing from the Bill & Melinda Gates Foundation, which donated over $20 million dollars for the construction of a new building dedicated to "expanding the horizons" of computer science in 2004.

Lesser known is the fact that donations

Art & Code is a highly interdisciplinary event at CMU that brings together more than 200 tinkerers and hackers, computational artists and designers, professional game developers, and leading researchers in the fields of computer vision, robotics and human-computer interaction.

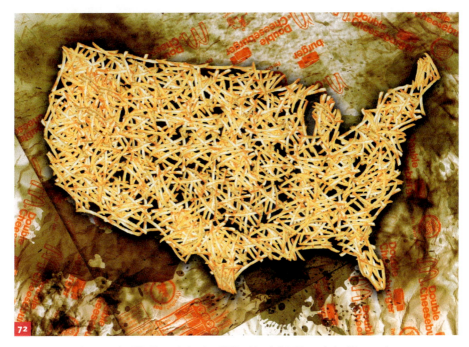

"One Nation Under Fries" by Ellis Kim, admitted to CMU with a full-tuition scholarship award.

made to CMU's computer science program benefit students pursuing art at CMU as well – as is evident in the recent rise of the number of Arts & Technologies courses offered at CMU. These courses, which aim to "narrow the gap between art and technology" are "stronger than ever," observes Edward H. Frank, vice president of Apple Inc. and a Carnegie Mellon life trustee. The demand for such hybridized coursework has risen sharply in recent years some speculate due to advances in communication technologies. It stands then that students who choose to take such courses may have more to gain than students who choose to take coursework in art alone.

Fact! *The video game industry is already one area where art and technology have merged. Today video games are not just for entertainment; they're also used for education and exercise.*

Fact! *70% of CMU grads find employment and 30% of CMU grads gain admission to graduate programs within their first year of graduation.*

As expected from a prestigious and well-funded university, CMU also makes sure its students have access to the latest technology. For example, before the start of each semester, the school updates all of its computers with the latest software and, if necessary, hardware. Additionally, select departments at CMU are also outfitted with advanced printing systems for laser-cutting architectural models, printing in large formats, and printing in 3D.

Tip! CMU awards additional scholarships and funding to the ten most talented students from every department every year. Also, if CMU approves a project proposed by one of these students, the student will be reimbursed for most of the material costs needed for her project by the school.

CMU WANTS ITS STUDENTS TO FAIL BETTER

What's more, via CMU's Student College, or StuCo, students may learn from the success of others to bring their own ideas to life. StuCo is a CMU initiative that provides one-credit, peer-to-peer learning experiences not available among the university's traditional course offerings.

"Falling into Disrepair" by Stephanie Park, admitted to CMU with a $190,000 scholarship award.

"Scarred for Life" by Hannah Kim, admitted to CMU with a $90,000 scholarship award.

"Visions of Perfection" by Regina Son, admitted to CMU with a full-tuition scholarship award.

In 2009, two StuCo students, Jesse Chorng and Elliott Curtis, who developed the first university course on sneaker culture also developed a project they called Sneakerology 101 in partnership with Reebok to manufacture and sell 101 pairs of limited edition "Reverse Jams" to benefit Pittsburgh's Hill House Association. The entrepreneurial and philanthropic pair applied knowledge gained from years of sneaker collecting and teaching fellow students about shoe design, manufacturing and marketing. The project was such a large success that even Time Magazine did a write-up on it.

This example reinforces the idea of "integrated educations" and demonstrates how important it is for students to work in an independent manner to make mistakes, identify solutions, and, as a result, learn to "fail better."

Fact! *CMU's undergraduate art program has gained a reputation for being notoriously rigorous. In fact, a significant percent of undergraduates get left back each year.*

WHAT CMU'S SCHOOL OF ART LOOKS FOR

CMU's School of Art is interested in students who demonstrate:

① **AN ENGAGEMENT WITH VARIOUS**

MATERIALS, IDEAS AND CONTEXTS
② CULTURAL AWARENESS AND AMBITION
③ TECHNICAL SKILLS
④ A WILLINGNESS TO EXPERIMENT AND ENGAGE IN PERSONAL RESEARCH
⑤ ABILITY TO WORK ON A WIDE RANGE OF ARTISTIC CONCERNS, IN DEPTH OR IN A SEQUENCE
⑥ STRONG SELF-MOTIVATION

Did you know? CMU doesn't take into consideration the grades you earned as a freshman in high school when reviewing applications to its undergraduate programs.

APPLICATION DEADLINES

EARLY DECISION DEADLINE
November 1 (Art & Architecture)
REGULAR DECISION DEADLINE
December 1 (Art & Architecture)
ART PORTFOLIO DEADLINE
January 15 (Art & Architecture)

Tip! *Although CMU's School of Architecture states that submitting a portfolio of "creative/inventive work" is optional, submitting a strong art portfolio will greatly increase a student's chances to be awarded scholarships.*

ADMISSIONS OFFICE

Carnegie Mellon University
Warner Hall
5000 Forbes Avenue
Pittsburgh, PA 15213-3890

Tip! *If you attend a campus tour prior to applying, CMU will add "1 bonus point" towards your application for admission.*

8

THE SCHOOL OF THE ART INSTITUTE OF CHICAGO

> " IN 2010, SAIC WAS NAMED THE "MOST INFLUENTIAL ART SCHOOL" BY ART CRITICS AT GENERAL INTEREST NEWS PUBLICATIONS FROM ACROSS THE U.S IN A SURVEY CONDUCTED BY THE NATIONAL ARTS JOURNALISM PROGRAM AT COLUMBIA UNIVERSITY. "

THE SCHOOL OF THE ART INSTITUTE OF CHICAGO

In 1871, a fire in Chicago known as "The Great Chicago Fire" spread quickly over the course of two days killing hundreds and burning close to four square miles of the city to the ground. Though the fire was one of the largest U.S. disasters of the 19th century, architects from around the nation banded together to help lift the city out of its ruined state. The combined efforts of many during this time served to spur Chicago's development into one of the most populous and economically important American cities today.

Now crowded with skyscrapers and distinctive architecture, the city has established for itself a strong foothold

SAIC has been recognized by Columbia University's National Arts Journalism survey as the most influential art school in the United States.

in tourism. The city touts multiple architecture tours daily, many of which operate along the Chicago River. Chicago is both economically advanced and a colorful urban city that offers many cultural attractions. As Obama's political hometown, Chicago also offers some of the nation's most highly ranked programs in law and liberal arts at Chicago University and Northwestern University and, of course, art at SAIC.

THE FOUNDING OF THE SCHOOL OF THE ART INSTITUTE OF CHICAGO

SAIC was originally founded in 1866 as The Chicago Academy of Design providing an education in design and the fine arts and exhibition opportunities for all of its students. In 1879, the school renamed itself The Chicago Academy of Fine Art then changed its name once again to the Art Institute of Chicago in 1882.

Then in 1893, Chicago was chosen to host a world fair celebrating the 400th anniversary of Columbus' landing. A new and enormous civic center was constructed to host the fair, which was titled the World's Columbian Exposition, and was later purchased by the Art Institute of Chicago. The AIC later divided the space to use for the purposes of a museum, which has become one of the most highly-trafficked museums in the country, and an art college, which in due course became known as the School of the Art Institute of Chicago.

Cloud Gate, a public sculpture by Indian-born British artist Anish Kapoor, said to have been inspired by liquid mercury, reflects and distorts Chicago's skyline.

Chicago's Ohio Street Beach is popular for the long stretch of swimming area that runs along its path and features bike rentals, beach chair rentals, and food vendors.

A LOOK AT WHY SAIC RANKS SO HIGHLY

In 2009, U.S. News & World Report ranked the SAIC the third best overall graduate program for fine arts in the U.S. Shortly after, SAIC was named the "most influential art school" by art critics at general interest news publications from across the U.S in a 2010 survey conducted by the National Arts Journalism Program at Columbia University – let's look at the most likley reasons why.

INTERDISCIPLINARY BFA CURRICULUMS FOR ALL

At SAIC, every undergraduate student works towards a Bachelors of Fine Arts regardless of their intended concentrations: students who center their course work on Architecture are encouraged to take courses in Fashion Design or Art Education while other

"Crown Fountain" by Jaume Plensa is an interactive work of public art and video sculpture featured in Chicago's Millennium Park, which is located in the Loop community area.

students majoring in Graphic Design are encouraged to take courses in Sculpture or 3D Animation. By doing so, SAIC produces more multidisciplinary graduates each year than any other undergraduate art program in the nation.

NO GRADES

All classes at SAIC are taught on a pass-fail basis to not only alleviate some of the pressures that stem from rigorous college-level coursework but to cultivate an open culture of creativity and collaboration. In place of graded exams, every student is required to present her work to different groups of faculty members at the end of every semester.

CHICAGO'S LARGEST MUSEUM AT YOUR DOORSTEP

The Art Institute of Chicago is physically connected – via a hallway – to SAIC providing its students with quick and exclusive access to one of Chicago's most renowned museums. The AIC houses the second largest collection of art and cultural artifacts in the nation

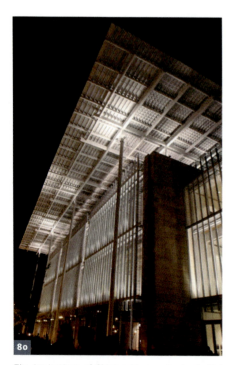

The Art Institute of Chicago Museum is closely tied to the School of the Art Institute of Chicago, which is the second largest art museum in the United States behind only the Metropolitan Museum of Art in New York City.

comprising over 270,000 works and includes some of the world's most important Impressionist and Post-impressionist paintings.

FREE MACBOOKS AND ADOBE FOR ALL

SAIC has recently announced that all entering freshmen receive free Macbooks and Adobe's latest Creative Suite; alluring incentives for the newly minted undergraduate. SAIC also offers spacious, bleeding-edge facilities and equipment for the aspiring photographer, filmmaker, designer and fine artist. In fact, almost half of SAIC's buildings are used for individual studio use so a much higher percentage of the student body are granted individual studio space early on in their undergraduate careers than at other art colleges.

THE CITY IS YOUR CAMPUS

The various attractions that lie in and around Chicago undoubtedly enrich every SAIC student's undergraduate experience. Millennium Park, a public park located in the Loop community area of Chicago along Michigan Lake, is within walking distance from the AIC and exhibits a diverse mix of public art year-round. Two of Millennium Park's

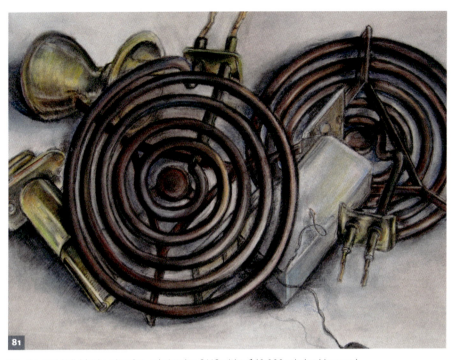

"Mechanical Still-life" by Alice Sun, admitted to SAIC with a $40,000 scholarship award.

most famous public art installations include one of Anish Kapoor's Cloud Gates, better known as "The Bean," and Jaume Plensa's Crown Fountain. Chicago's Field Museum, which houses the largest collection of dinosaur fossils in the world, and the John G. Shedd Aquarium, which was the largest aquarium in the U.S. up until 2005, are also close-by. Both attractions are great places from which students may gain even more inspiration and knowledge.

THE SAIC ADVANTAGE

Today, SAIC is separated into a range of departments including Arts Administration and Policy, Architecture, Architecture and Interior, Art Education, Art History, Theory and Criticism, Art and Technology, Art Therapy, Ceramics, Emerging Technologies for Design, Fashion Design, Textile Design, Film, Video and New Media. As an SAIC student, you'll be encouraged by the school to reach across department lines when scheduling coursework for the purposes of self-expansion and a farther-reaching educational experience.

Undergraduate degrees include Bachelors Degrees in Visual and Critical

"360" by Alex Khomyakov, admitted to SAIC with a $44,000 scholarship award.

Studies and Interior Architecture. Most other students graduate from SAIC with a Bachelors Degree in Fine Arts, or a BFA. Additionally, SAIC also offers BFA degrees that place emphases on Art Education, Art History, Art Theory & Criticism, or Writing. Lastly, SAIC also offers one dual BA/BFA degree that equally emphasizes practice and theory.

During foundation year, required coursework includes classes in Art Conservation, Painting and Drawing, Performance, Photo, Sculpture, Sound, Visual Communication, Visual Critique, and Writing.

Graduate degrees are offered in Architecture, Architecture with an Emphasis in Interior Architecture, Arts Administration and Policy, Art Education, Art Therapy, Modern Art History, Theory and Criticism, New Arts Journalism, Art Education, Visual and Critical Studies, Designed Objects, Fashion, Studio Writing, and Historic Preservation. Dual degrees are available for Modern Art History, Theory and Criticism, and Arts Administration and Policy majors.

SAIC admits students on a rolling basis allowing students to apply whenever

"Slices of Time" by Jennifer Kim, admitted to SAIC with a $72,000 scholarship award.

their art portfolio and application materials are ready for submission. However, if students are looking to apply for merit scholarships, all required materials must be submitted by SAIC's deadline; Merit scholarships at SAIC are awarded according to the strength of a student's portfolio rather than the strength of her grades. When applying for a merit scholarship, it is very important that you submit a series of 10 artworks that share a theme, are carefully arranged and are cohesively represented. When your portfolio is ready for submission, affix a label to it identifying it as a merit scholarship entry. SAIC accepts both digital and printed formats. If you decide to present your portfolio via prints, print only on heavy, archival photo paper.

APPLICATION DEADLINES

EARLY DECISION DEADLINE
January 3
PRIORITY DECISION DEADLINE
February 15

ADMISSIONS OFFICE

School of the Art Institute of Chicago
Admissions Office
36 South Wabash, Suite 1201
Chicago, IL 60603

9

NEW YORK UNIVERSITY

> " NYU HAS 3 PORTAL CAMPUSES: ONE IN THE HEART OF MANHATTAN'S GREENWICH VILLAGE, ONE IN THE RAPIDLY GROWING MIDDLE EASTERN CITY OF ABU DHABI, AND A THIRD OPENING IN SHANGHAI IN 2013. "

NEW YORK UNIVERSITY

Founded in 1831 by Albert Gallatin, Treasury Secretary to U.S. Presidents Thomas Jefferson and James Madison, New York University, or NYU, is one of the largest private universities in the United States comprising more than 18 schools, colleges, and institutes, located in six centers throughout Manhattan and Downtown Brooklyn, as well as a dozen other sites around the world.

Across its 18 schools and colleges, NYU collectively offers over 230 programs and 4,500 courses that enroll close to 20,282 undergraduates every semester.

Many of NYU's programs are regularly ranked within the top 10 worldwide -

NYU's main campus is situated in the neighborhood of Greenwich Village in Manhattan. Founded in 1831, NYU is one of the largest private, nonprofit institutions of higher education in the United States.

most notably its programs in business, law and art. In fact, NYU counts 34 Nobel Prize winners, 3 Abel Prize winners, 10 National Medal of Science recipients, 16 Pulitzer Prize winners, 21 Academy Award winners, and Emmy,

Grammy, and Tony Award winners.

GLOBAL INTEGRATION AT NYU

NYU has 3 portal campuses: one in the heart of Manhattan's Greenwich Village, one in the rapidly growing Middle Eastern city of Abu Dhabi, and a third opening in Shanghai in 2013. And according to The Institute of International Education's annual Open Doors Report, NYU has been sending more students abroad than any other institution in the U.S. for the past five years.

The university's main campus offers over 4,500 courses through 11 different colleges:

① **COLLEGE OF ARTS AND SCIENCE**
② **LIBERAL STUDIES**
③ **LEONARD N. STERN SCHOOL OF BUSINESS**
④ **STEINHARDT SCHOOL OF CULTURE, EDUCATION, AND HUMAN DEVELOPMENT**
⑤ **TISCH SCHOOL OF THE ARTS**
⑥ **GALLATIN SCHOOL OF INDIVIDUALIZED STUDY**
⑦ **SILVER SCHOOL OF SOCIAL WORK**
⑧ **PRESTON ROBERT TISCH CENTER FOR HOSPITALITY, TOURISM, AND SPORTS**

The Leonard N. Stern School of Business (commonly known as The Stern School, NYU Stern, or simply Stern) is New York University's business school. NYU Stern is constantly ranked within the top 10 best business schools in the United States, and within the top 20 best business schools in the world.

Washington Square Park is one of the best-known of New York City's 1,900 public parks. The park's fountain area has long been one of the city's popular spots for residents and tourists with most of the buildings surrounding the park now belonging to New York University, but many of which have at one time served as homes and studios for artists.

MANAGEMENT

⑨ **COLLEGE OF NURSING**

⑩ **NYU-POLY**

⑪ **PAUL MCGHEE DIVISION FOR NON-TRADITIONAL UNDERGRADUATES**

Fact! As of 2007, NYU has the seventh-largest university housing system in the U.S. with approximately 12,500 residents in 19 dormitories.

A CITY FOR ARTISTS

Artists have been drawn into New York City by opportunity for years as the city funds the arts with a larger annual budget than the National Endowment for the Arts and because the city serves as a global center for the international art market.

The industry is clustered in neighborhoods known for their art galleries, such as Chelsea and SoHo, where dealers representing both established and emerging artists compete for sales with bigger exhibition spaces, better locations, and stronger connections to museums and collectors.

Enriching and countering this mainstream commercial movement is the constant flux of underground movements, such as lowbrow art and street art, which engendered such artists as Keith Haring and Jean-Michel Basquiat, and continue to add visual texture and life to the atmosphere of the city.

Did you know? Long Island City (LIC) in Queens is a rapidly flourishing art scene in

New York City, serving as home to the largest concentration of arts institutions outside of Manhattan. Its abundance of industrial warehouses provide ample studio and exhibition space for many renowned artists, museums and galleries.

NYU'S ART PROGRAM OPTIONS

Within New York City's cosmopolitan environment, NYU serves as a home for visual artists where they can work side by side with acclaimed performers, scientists, theorists, and philosophers to creatively cross the bounds of many different disciplines.

NYU Steinhardt's Department of Art and Art Professions' BFA and MFA programs in studio art are interdisciplinary, foster discussion-centered learning, and combine cultural theory with facilities in painting, sculpture, photography, computer art and design, video, performance, ceramics, metal-smithing, installation, curatorial projects, and an environmental health clinic. The department's MA programs include Art Education, Visual Arts Administration, Costume Studies, and Art Therapy.

Did you know? *Internationally renowned artist*

NYU has 3 portal campuses: one in the heart of Manhattan's Greenwich Village, one in the rapidly growing Middle Eastern city of Abu Dhabi, and a third opening in Shanghai in 2013.

"Violent Ultimatum" by Jenn Park, admitted to NYU with a $120,000 scholarship award.

"The Train Station" by Erin Sul, admitted to NYU's Studio Art Program.

Kiki Smith teaches undergraduate and graduate courses at NYU as a part-time professor.

NYU'S GLOBAL VISUAL ART MINOR

The Global Visual Art Minor brings the hands-on experience of international art to students across the university. This minor provides an in-depth understanding of diverse cultures by combining Art History and Studio Art classes in New York with studio art courses in Berlin, Ghana, Florence, Prague, Shanghai, or Abu Dhabi!

Did you know? *NYU's Gallatin School of Individualized Study, a small, experimental college within New York University, has been giving NYU students the opportunity to design curriculums of study tailored to their own needs and interests for more than 30 years.*

NYU'S TICKET CENTRAL

NYU Ticket Central is NYU's clearinghouse for tickets to the movies, Broadway and Off-Broadway shows, sporting events, musical concerts and more, all at a reduced price. NYU Ticket Central has built a reputation for itself as being able to reach a large audience in a moment's notice. Each week, numerous theatre producers and promoters rely on Ticket Central to help them fill their houses. NYU students have enjoyed free admission to preview performances of many Broadway, Off-Broadway shows, and The NYC Ballet, and tickets to NY Knicks basketball games at Madison Square Garden for as low as $12 and NY Yankees and Mets baseball games for as low as $6!

ON GAINING ADMISSION TO NYU

NYU Steinhardt's Department of Art and Art Professions' looks for applicants with GPAs of 3.8 or higher, and SAT scores of 2000 or higher. NYU's rates of acceptance for early and regular decision applicants are 39% and 30% respectively.

In general, it is also important to submit a well-rounded application bolstered by demonstrations of leadership, certificates of awards and honors, a solid record of involvement in volunteer activities, and a developed concept-driven art portfolio.

What differentiates NYU's art admissions process is its required 1-page artist statement which requires applicants to describe their goals as an artist; artistic influences, including two contemporary artists who are nationally or internationally recognized (these artists should have created new work within the past 20 years and they should be represented in major art museums or art galleries which feature contemporary visual artists); background and interests, including previous art training, and films, literature, or music you enjoy and how they relate to your art work; and what

"Simulacrum" by Fabiana Um, admitted to NYU with a $104,000 scholarship award.

you hope to gain from studying in the studio art program at NYU.

Tip! When writing about your artistic influences, select contemporary artists whose works relate either visually or conceptually to your own.

DEADLINES

EARLY APPLICATION DEADLINE
November 1

EARLY PORTFOLIO DEADLINE
November 8

REGULAR APPLICATION DEADLINE
January 1

REGULAR PORTFOLIO DEADLINE
January 8

ADMISSIONS OFFICE
Office of Undergraduate Admissions
New York University
655 Broadway, 11th Floor
New York, NY 10012

ART STATEMENTS AND PORTFOLIOS SHOULD BE SENT DIRECTLY TO:
Student Services Counselor
New York University,
The Steinhardt School
Dept of Art & Art Professions
34 Stuyvesant Street
New York, NY 10003

"The Outbreak" by Eunah Kim, admitted early to NYU's Studio Art Program.

ABOUT THE AUTHOR
WOOK CHOI

Wook Choi is an accomplished artist, educator, newspaper columnist, art portfolio consultant, art dealer, and the Founder and Director of Oogie Art, a New York City based Art Portfolio Prep School with 3 locations in and around Manhattan, which guides young artists, in the words of Mayor Michael Bloomberg, to "greater heights of artistic creation."

After earning a B.F.A. from Hong-ik University and an M.A. from New York University, Wook won numerous awards as an artist and has exhibited in 8 solo shows and 35 group shows in Europe, US, China, and Korea. With curatorial experience, she partnered with Fiorella la Lumia Lattuada to establish Wook & Lattuada Art Galleries in Manhattan and Milan, which currently house the largest collection (124 pieces) of Futurist works in the world; hold works by Pablo Picasso, Lucio Fontana, Mimmo Rotella, Amedeo Modigliani, Umberto Boccioni, and Vassily Kandinsky; and focus on exhibiting important work by both internationally established and emerging contemporary artists each year.

She opened her first art academy at the age of twenty-one and has since taught at various institutions around the world accruing over 28 years of teaching experience. As an art instructor, she has received nation-wide recognition for her creative methods from eminent persons

Once a year, Wook creates pre-college volunteer programs that aim to effect lasting change through art. For more information, visit www.wookchoi.com.

and organizations including, but not limited to, the former first lady, Laura Bush; the New York Commissioner of Education, Richard P. Mills; US Congress member, Jerrold Nadler; the Alliance for Young Artists; the National Foundation for the Advancement in the Arts; and the Marie Walsh Sharpe Foundation.

For her school, Oogie Art, she has pioneered far-reaching Global Art Initiatives™, which afford her students extraordinary experiences in Rome, Florence, Venice, Milan, London, Paris, Barcelona, Kuala Lumpur, Chiang Mai, Incheon, New York City, Chicago, and other major cities around the world; Young Artist Volunteer Programs™, which help create scholarships for abandoned, abused and orphaned children living abroad; Artist Mentoring Programs™, which pair young artists with established New York City designers, architects and artists as mentors; and Business of Design Programs™, which allow her students to design, manufacture, distribute, market, and sell their own product design ideas.

Through art and her innovative programs, her students are able to gain admission to top programs at

Harvard, Brown, UPenn, Stanford, Columbia, Princeton, Dartmouth, Duke, Georgetown, Cornell, the Cooper Union, and many other highly-ranked colleges with scholarships each year. In fact, her students have been awarded over $28.5 million in scholarship awards over the past decade.

Wook has written dozens of articles on art education, which have been published in a variety of print and online publications on over a hundred different occasions, and she continues to write columns for various publications today.

She speaks regularly at education events around the world. For a full list of events and dates, click to www.wookchoi.com.

For those seeking individualized guidance with the development of their art portfolios, Wook can be reached via email at wook@wookchoi.com.

Wook lives in Manhattan with her eleven-year-old son, Aron, who is in the process of publishing his first book.

NOTES

PHOTO CREDITS

ALL IMAGES USED UNDER A CREATIVE COMMONS ATTRIBUTION-SHAREALIKE LICENSE.
http://creativecommons.org/licenses/by-sa/2.0/deed.en

01	"Samsung Smart TV" taken on January 6, 2011 by "ETC@USA"
02	"Apple iPad Event" taken on January 27, 2010 by Matt Buchanan
03	"Coco Chanel" taken on November 29, 2004 by "Teadrinker"
04	"Kartell LaMarie" taken on February 12, 2010 by "Conference Basics"
05	"Guggenheim Bilbao" taken on May 25, 2008 "Aherrero"
06	"Harvard College Graduates" taken on May 25, 2010 by "Zilinsky"
07	Courtney Wong, an Oogie Art student, with her mentor, Sally Taylor
08	"Outside Columbia University Library" taken on July 2, 2011 by Alex Proimos
24	"Cooper Union New Academic Building" taken on September 2, 2011 by "Jules Antonio"
25	"Classroom 104, the 'Fishbowl'" taken on September 28, 2009 by "JohnRH4"
27	"School of Art Discussion " taken on September 28, 2009 by "JohnRH4"
29	"Atrium, Cooper Union New Academic Building" taken on August 31, 2010 by "Takomabibelot"
30	"I_09A7 College Hill - The College Building/Franklin House Hotel (1822) (RISD) - 2 College Street - Detail" taken on August 20, 1990 by Will Hart
31	"Art class, Rhode Island School of Design, Providence, 7th. April 2011" taken on April 8, 2011 by Phillip Capper
32	"Brown University Quad" taken on July 14, 2007 by "thurdl01"
33	"risd beach mats" taken on July 27, 2005 by Johanna Abzug
38	"Cornell tower" taken on May 15, 2009 by Devin Hunter
39	"Cornell Central Campus in Snow" taken on December 18, 2005 by "Hobbes vs Boyle"
45	"Pratt Institute" taken on July 19, 2008 by "angela n."
46	"Hanging" taken on December 30, 2007 by Sarah Le Clerc

47	"Pratt Institute" taken on July 19, 2008 by "angela n."
48	"Benches, Pratt Institute" taken on June 6, 2011 by "prattHAD"
54	"Where it all happens B/W" taken on May 30, 2008 by Maureen Didde
55	"Sidewalk Catwalk by Nanette Lepore" taken on June 24, 2010 by "nycstreets"
62	"SVA Big Crit" taken on November 19, 2007 by "FEARstyle"
65	"Vimeo Awards 10/9/10" taken on October 9, 2010 by Mindy Bond
78	"CMU from 36th floor of the Cathedral of Learning" taken on August 26, 2009 by "chloester"
69	"Entering ETC" taken on April 8, 2008 by Alberto D'Ottavi
70	"walking to the sky" taken on April 19, 2008 by "saeru"
71	"DSC_3932" taken on November 8, 2009 by Ecin Krispie
76	"School of the Art Institute of Chicago" taken on January 7, 2012 by "Terry Robinson"
77	"Chicago (ILL), Millennium Park, Cloud Gate : " the Bean " Anish Kapoor 2004-06" taken on June 9, 2010 by "vincent [star]"
78	"chicago skyline from navy pier beach" taken on July 23, 2005 by Julian Jensen
79	"Millenium Park" taken on August 6, 2004 by Chris Brown
80	"The Art Institute of Chicago - Sept 2010" taken on September 2, 2010 by
84	"mycatfredisfat"
86	"NYU commencement 2007" taken on May 11, 2007 by Jeffrey Bary
87	"Washington Square Park Pano" taken on June 11, 2011 by Joe Hall
	"Around NYU, Start of the Fall Semester" taken on September 7, 2006 by Barry Solow